The Armchair Birder

DISCOVERING
the SECRET LIVES

The Armchair Birder

of FAMILIAR BIRDS

JOHN YOW

The University *of* North Carolina Press
Chapel Hill

This book was published with the assistance of the Blythe Family Fund of the University of North Carolina Press.

© 2009 by JOHN YOW
Designed by Kimberly Bryant
Set in Whitman and Bickham by
Tseng Information Systems, Inc.
Manufactured in the United States of America

The paper in this book meets the guidelines for permanence and durability of the Committee on Production Guidelines for Book Longevity of the Council on Library Resources.

The University of North Carolina Press has been a member of the Green Press Initiative since 2003.

LIBRARY OF CONGRESS
CATALOGING-IN-PUBLICATION DATA
Yow, John.
The armchair birder : discovering the secret lives of familiar birds / by John Yow.
p. cm.
Includes bibliographical references and index.
ISBN 978-0-8078-3279-0 (cloth : alk. paper)
1. Birds. 2. Bird watching. I. Title.
QL673.Y69 2009
598.0973—dc22

2008031979

cloth   13 12 11 10 09   5 4 3 2 1

This book is dedicated,
with affection and admiration, *to my father.*

CONTENTS

INTRODUCTION

The designation "armchair birder" signals no achievement and confers no distinction. I can't claim to have driven 300 miles in the middle of the night to see the avocets at dawn on Delaware Bay. As for my "life list," you could just about get the whole thing on a cocktail napkin.

What I do, mostly, is hang feeders and watch the birds that come to me. I listen to their songs and sometimes succeed in figuring out which bird is singing which tune. I observe what I can of their behavior. If a bird happens to wander in that I haven't seen before, it's a big day. I'm like, as Keats says, "some watcher of the skies / When a new planet swims into his ken."

Following family tradition, I've always hung a bird feeder or two, but my skies got bigger ten years ago when my wife and daughter and I moved from the suburbs to the country. I began seeing woodland birds I'd only seen pictures of—tanagers, indigo buntings, pileated woodpeckers, the shy and retiring yellow-billed cuckoo. The first spring we were here, I looked out the window and dropped my spoon into my cereal bowl. A rose-breasted grosbeak was sitting on the feeder. My goodness—Peterson's cover bird, not twenty feet away.

Again, though, you don't have to live in the woods to be an armchair birder. On the other hand, if your interest extends beyond the boundaries of your own property, you are permitted to get out of your chair—temporarily anyway. I confess to having seen swallow-tailed kites in the Florida panhandle, frigate birds circling around a highrise hotel in Cancun, and black skimmers on the Georgia coast. At a bird sanctuary in Jamaica, the spectacular "doctor-bird" perched on my finger and sipped sugar water from a drip-bottle.

But the armchair birder doesn't have to go anywhere. Because here's the thing: Reading is encouraged. Birds, after all, are downright remarkable creatures, and there's only so much I'm going to find out by watching the chickadees, nuthatches, and titmice that come to the feeder all year-round. So, establishing my armchair status, I have an ever-expanding bookshelf that includes, among other things, some Audubon, some Forbush, and a dozen or so volumes of Arthur Cleveland Bent's *Life Histories* series. I skim through the publications of a couple of bird organizations I've given a few dollars to. Thanks to the folks at the Cornell Lab of Ornithology, I can subscribe to *The Birds of North America Online*, an unbelievable resource.

The more I find out, of course, the more I want to know. There's no end to the mystery and wonder of bird behavior. Sure, part of me wants to be out in the field, on top of Kennesaw Mountain at the break of day watching the warbler migration or tromping through the swampy forests of southeast Arkansas to confirm the reappearance of the majestic ivory-billed woodpecker. But the professionals have done the legwork, and more power to them. As an armchair birder, I accept a humbler role: If I can't paint like Audubon, maybe I can put his pictures in new frames.

You understand, then, that this book is no field guide. The forty birds I've concentrated on here are widely familiar, and chances are good that you can already identify most if not all of them. But, if you're like me, identifying them is the beginning, not the end, of the journey. If you're like me, knowing what they look like just whets your appetite for knowing what they're up to. Sitting in my armchair, I've discovered some of that less familiar information.

Of course, I'm working on the assumption that you are like me: that you're fascinated by birds like I am; that your eyes are quick to follow any shadow flitting through the tree limbs; that on clear winter days your ears strain toward the high-up, far-off gabbling of sandhill cranes; and — not least important — that you're predisposed to find some pleasure in these pages.

A NOTE ON THE SOURCES

A traditional bibliography, with some annotation, is supplied at the end of the book, but since I didn't want to burden the text with the distracting apparatus of footnotes, I thought readers might appreciate a prefatory note about a few of the sources that I used most frequently.

Arthur Cleveland Bent is the author/compiler/editor of the incredible twenty-one-volume *Life Histories of North American Birds*. Bent was close to the completion of volume 20 and had begun to compile volume 21 when he died at his home in Taunton, Massachusetts, in 1958 at the age of eighty-eight. Bent himself wrote many of the entries in these volumes, but some were contributed by other experts, notably Winsor Marrett Tyler. Whoever the author, the essays also depend heavily on the field notes of a wide variety of correspondents. As a result, my essays might refer to Bent or to Tyler or to one of Bent's correspondents or to *Life Histories*; in any case, it's all the same magnificent resource. By the way, the final volume was completed by Oliver Austin, whose own book, *Birds of the World*, provided another important source for my work.

Edward Howe Forbush (1858–1929), who became the Massachusetts state ornithologist in 1908 and subsequently founded the Massachusetts Audubon Society, is the author of the three-volume *Birds of Massachusetts and Other New England States*. The work I refer to, *A Natural History of American Birds of Eastern and Central North America*, is an abridgment of the three-volume work, with additional material supplied by John Bichard May. The abridgment retains the wonderful illustrations by Louis Agassiz Fuertes and Allan Brooks, along with four additional plates by Roger Tory Peterson.

John James Audubon (1785–1851), best known as the artist who created *Birds of America*, was also an accomplished and highly entertaining writer. His prose masterpiece is his five-volume *Ornithological Biography*, published in the 1830s to accompany the artwork. The copies of this work that I located via the Internet were too expensive for me, so I got most of what I needed by reading microfiche at the local university library. There are also excerpts from the *Biography* in the readily available *Audubon: Writings and Drawings*.

Finally, to bring my research into the twenty-first century (not to mention the second half of the twentieth), I depended heavily on *The Birds of North America Online*. The print version of this comprehensive resource (eighteen volumes covering 716 species), edited by Drs. Alan Poole and Frank Gill, appeared in 2002, the culmination of a ten-year effort on the part of the American Ornithologists' Union, the Cornell Lab of Ornithology, and the Academy of Natural Sciences. Now, happily, thanks to the Cornell Lab, the whole thing, with audio, video, and recurrent updating, is available online—for a small annual subscription fee.

The Armchair Birder

Spring

(overleaf) *Detail view of Mourning Dove (John James Audubon,*
The Birds of America, vols. 1–4, Special Collections, University Library
System, University of Pittsburgh)

Carolina Wren

Thryothorus ludovicianus

> *All things fall and are built again,*
> *And those that build them again are gay.*
> —*William Butler Yeats, "Lapis Lazuli"*

I suspect Yeats had weightier matters in mind when he wrote those lines, but for me they epitomize the delightful, curious Carolina wren, a bird that always seems to be either building or singing, if not both at the same time. Here in the South, they might raise three broods, all in different nests, during the course of the season. Plus, they build nests, or at least parts of nests, that they never use. And they build *anywhere*.

Anywhere, that is, except in the wren box June White gave me three years ago. The all-time record for level of interest in the box was set this past spring when a wren lit on the little perch outside the entrance hole, took a look inside, and flew away. But that's okay, better than okay, because left to its own devices, the wren will build in places much more interesting than inside a boring old bird box.

Last year the wrens exceeded expectations by somehow constructing their nest on top of the business end of a push broom that leaned into the dim corner of the garage. It was a typically unprepossessing mélange of leaf litter, twigs, moss, rootlets, grass, and such, with a tunnel-like entrance (thus the wrens' family name, "troglodyte") that, for me, was a little lower than eye high. Carolina wrens get skittish when people come around, and at first the mom would dart out—always startling—whenever we walked into the garage. But the female is also a "tight sitter" when hatching time approaches, so eventually she would ignore us, even let us peer inside, during our comings and goings.

One day I wanted a better look at how things were progressing in there, so I took my flashlight out, walked up close, and clicked on the beam. *WHOA!* The tangle of leaves and twigs that had been their nest was all tangled up in snake. I jumped back about ten feet. It

looked like a copperhead. (Funny how many snakes, when you walk up on them unawares, look like a copperhead.) I approached again, took a more careful look, and decided that it didn't look quite so much like a copperhead after all. I went inside, consulted my book, and concluded that it was actually the nonvenomous and much-maligned milk snake. I used my long walking stick to lift it down onto the ground and, in the better light, confirmed its identity. The markings were clear enough, but another detail helped: The only part of its body fat enough to be a copperhead was one distended lump right in the middle where, no doubt, either some little baby wrens or some little wren's eggs were being digested. The snake was so lethargic from its meal, it took me ten minutes to stick-shoo it across the driveway and into the woods.

Did the parents grieve their loss? Maybe, but the wren is not a bird to dwell in sadness. I threw away their broom-end nest to discourage them from trying that spot again, and within a day or two I heard them out my office window singing their hearts out. It looked like they might be building in the recesses of the upturned root-ball just off the edge of the yard where a tree blew down a few years back. That suited me fine, since it was another place I figured to be able to get a look at. But a couple of days later, damned if I didn't see building activity on top of that same broom in the garage. I did what I should've done in the first place and moved it out of there, and the next thing we knew, the wrens were flying in and out of the asparagus fern Dede had just hung on the front porch.

I understood that Dede's objections were perfunctory, that deep in her heart she was delighted to have a family of wrens making their home in her fern. The wrens understood it, too, and that's where they built nest no. 2—like the first, so haphazard on the outside but so lovingly crafted inside. Clambering up onto the porch rail with my flashlight, I soon saw the five little eggs, pale off-white with their dusting of brown spots. But for several days I never saw the female

Carolina Wren (John James Audubon, The Birds of America, vols. 1–4, Special Collections, University Library System, University of Pittsburgh)

flying in and out—or the male coming to feed her if she was, in fact, in there. Dede and I persisted in our habit of sitting out on the porch at the end of the day, pulling our rockers as far away from the fern as we could, and finally our vigil was rewarded. As the afternoon light faded, one of the wrens took up a position on the rail at the far end of the porch and sat there twitching, as though waiting impatiently for us to get the hell away. Which we did.

The next night, around eight o'clock, we heard the loud trill (*chier-r-r, chier-r-r*) from the far side of the driveway and thought that maybe the male was coming to feed his mate or take a turn on the nest. Sure enough, we heard a stirring and turned to see, in the dim light, one of the wrens dive into the nest. I think that, hearing the call, the female came out, saw us there, and dove back in. Meanwhile the call continued, and, again, we went inside to get out of the way.

The next day my curiosity got the better of me, and in the late morning I climbed back up on the porch rail and shone my light down inside. There she was, incubating her little heart out, sitting tight even with my big moon face hovering right outside her entryway.

We spent the next two weeks watching the parents feed the young. They signaled their annoyance by flying toward the nest with an insect in their bill and then, seeing us, veering off to land nearby—on the porch rail, maybe, or sideways on the porch-swing chain. But it was too late for them to pick up and move now, so after the brief detour they would proceed on to the nest, where they were met by the small twittering clamor of their babies. Imagine how gratified I was to watch the parents leave the nest, fly out to my little vegetable garden, then return with a beak full of bug that would otherwise have been devouring my tomato plants.

The feeding was a routine I didn't want to intrude upon, but, on the other hand, I did want to see the young leave the nest. We had been watching pretty regularly when, on an evening in early June, we noticed the nest was quiet. I checked the next morning and found it empty. Had they fledged successfully, or had disaster struck again? When they're ready to leave the nest, do they just up and go in an hour's time? I didn't know. But a few days later I saw a reassuring sight. A disheveled little wren was in the low limb of a poplar tree outside my window, stuttering over its trill note as if it hadn't quite mastered it yet, bobbing its head like crazy as it worked to get it right. No reason in the world for me not to believe that it was one of our asparagus-fern fledglings.

Have I made clear how much I love this bird—this tiny Carolina wren with its big jubilant song? "One of our great singers," writes Arthur Cleveland Bent in praise of the beautiful voice that rings out in town and country. Everybody has a favorite translation: *tea-kettle, tea-kettle, tea-kettle* or *sweet William, sweet William, sweet William* or even *Richelieu, Richelieu, Richelieu*. My own rendering is *jibberty, jibberty, jibberty,* which, though lacking the dignity of actual language, at least more or less rhymes with Audubon's version: *come-to-me, come-to-me, come-to-me.* "When satiated with food," he writes, "or fatigued with [its] multiplied exertions, the little fellow stops, droops his tail, and sings with great energy a short ditty . . . so loud, and yet so mellow, that it is always agreeable to listen to them."

Unlike their promiscuous cousin the house wren,* Carolina wrens bond for the duration of the season (if not for life), so from late winter to late summer the same two birds build and sing and raise their young together. The faithful male does his fair share, taking care to

---

*Slightly smaller than the Carolina wren and also lacking Carolina's conspicuous white eyebrow, the house wren is an even more prodigious builder than its cousin. Some say he courts by nest-building, offering his prospective mate a choice of the several nests he has constructed. Others believe the extra nests are built to dupe the cowbird into laying in them rather than in the real nest. Still others believe he likes to have an extra nest for his own nighttime sleeping chamber.

What's clear is that with so many nests available, the house wren sometimes takes on a second mate, which is, of course, a testament not to promiscuity but, rather, to his urgent reproductive instinct. In fact, says Bent, an unattached male will continue to build nests all season long, and, even more remarkable, pairs that have failed to reproduce, or individuals without a mate, have been known to feed the young, or even the adults, of other species. In one case on record, a house wren brought caterpillars to a nesting grosbeak, "which she usually proceeded to feed to her young, but was not above occasionally ingesting for herself."

see that the first brood fledges successfully while the female moves on to lay her second set of eggs in a nest the male has built for the purpose. In some instances, the young of the first mating hang around also and help in the feeding of their younger generation of siblings.

When the long season comes to an end, the wrens don't migrate but seem to disperse. No longer looking for an old coat pocket or discarded coffee cup to build in, they depart from porch and garage and take to the woods. And, for the time being, as the leaves turn and fall, their lovely voice is stilled.

But then the New Year comes in, and on those short, cold, gray days when I might otherwise be depressed, something is stirring outside my window. *Jibberty! Jibberty! Jibberty!* The tireless little bundle of bright rusty brown is singing from the top of the root-ball. Now it's on the ground, then up the trunk of the oak tree to the suet feeder (which I have refilled now that the squirrels have laid by their own store of food for the winter). It tears off more than it can swallow, and the chunk falls to the ground, where a second wren suddenly appears.

A mated pair already, at the end of January? The male and female look so much alike that it's impossible to say, but it doesn't matter. The wrens are singing. Spring will come.

....

Eastern Phoebe
Sayornis phoebe

One of my favorite "bird books" is the classic *Birds of the South*, by the longtime North Carolina naturalist Charlotte Hilton Green, published in 1933. Not surprisingly, the book has a quaintness about it now, at least in part because it employed the old-fashioned device of beginning each piece with a poem about the bird under discussion. Before it was resuscitated by the modernists in the early part of the twentieth century, American poetry itself was quaint, and most of the poems Green chooses sound downright silly today, stuffed with poetic diction and marching along in their precisely measured iambs and anapests. In short, they are much more about themselves than about the bird they purport to describe.

There is one exception—a quatrain about the phoebe written by James Russell Lowell. Here it is:

Phoebe is all it has to say
In plaintive cadence o'er and o'er,
Like children that have lost their way
And know their names, but nothing more.

You only have to listen to the phoebe for a day or two to know how perfect that is.

Of course, the phoebe doesn't exactly *say* "phoebe." It squeaks it or, perhaps, squeezes it. I have to tell you that even when I was young and my hearing was good, I was still pretty much tone deaf, so I don't usually tread in these waters. When it comes to clever human analogues for birds' songs, I'm a follower, not a leader. If you say the white-throated sparrow is singing *Old Sam Peabody Peabody Peabody*, I'd be the last to argue with you. But with the phoebe I had something of an epiphany. Exactly what this bird sounds like suddenly came to me: a little rubber ducky, especially in the hands of a hyperactive child. Go ahead, squeeze it: *phoebe, phoebe, phoebe.*

Don't get me wrong. I love the phoebe. It has become our own harbinger of spring, arriving in mid-February even before the first

forsythia blossoms. From that point on, we don't worry about setting the radio-alarm. It's *phoebe, phoebe, phoebe* from the moment the sky begins to brighten. (Incidentally, the male has more in mind than announcing daybreak. His early morning song summons the female, and their quick, scarcely noticeable courtship is consummated. What's more, that's his one chance; if he tries to get something going later in the day, she's not having any.)

Once the little flycatcher has rousted us out of bed, it keeps us entertained by perching on the porch rail in front or the deck rail in back, twitching its tail side to side, then darting off to snatch a morsel of breakfast out of the air. The phoebe scores no points for gay apparel ("dull in plumage with scarcely a field mark," says Bent's *Life Histories*), but I kind of like the dark little cap with its tousled look, the alert dark eyes, and the black, bug-catching bill. Since its breeding range extends no farther south than Atlanta, I feel fortunate to have this bird as a summer resident.

And make no mistake: The phoebe loves our log house, with its variety of choice nesting sites. Two years ago a pair built their nest on top of one of the rafters on the front porch. Well, she built it; nest-building is the female's job, though the male often keeps her company. Like the typical phoebe nest, it was mostly mud, with grass and other plant fibers mixed in. Phoebes love to use moss, too, when they can find it, and I've got plenty of that. (One of my landscaping goals, as a matter of fact, is to have an all-moss yard. I asked writer and naturalist June White what might promote moss-spread, and she told me to spray it with buttermilk. I confess I haven't acted on that recommendation.) Plus, hymenoptera—bees and wasps—are a mainstay of the phoebe's almost entirely insect diet, and Lord knows I've got plenty of those. Professor F. E. L. Beal, the expert on birds' feeding habits on whom Bent depends throughout *Life Histories*, says the phoebe should be welcome wherever it decides to build: "It pays ample rent for its accommodations."

Eastern Phoebe (John James Audubon, The Birds of America, *vols. 1–4, Special Collections, University Library System, University of Pittsburgh*) *spring*

The rafter on which that nest sat was tucked right beneath the porch roof, so I couldn't see down into it. I assume the female laid her five or six eggs inside it, but I never saw any feeding activity or heard from the young, so I don't know whether the nest was successful. I had better luck last year, when a pair (the same pair?) opted for the other side of the house and built on a narrow beam underneath the deck. Actually, I couldn't look down into this one either, until it occurred to me to hold Dede's mirror above it. I saw the tiny, just-hatched chicks stirring feebly and watched the parents hunt and gather for several days. I didn't see the fledglings leave the nest but have no reason to suppose that they didn't. (A few weeks later, though, I was given a reason to assume the worst when I noticed that the mother was back on the nest, and after investigating, I found another set of five tiny white eggs inside. Does that mean the first brood didn't make it? I wondered. No, it doesn't. The phoebe is "double brooded," and once the first set of children has fledged, the parents are at it again.)

But then I had another worry. I found out that while the phoebe does sometimes return to the same nest for a second brood, she's really better off if she builds a new one. The old one is likely to be infested with parasites, said to be the bird's worst enemy. Green says this threat is particularly dire when the phoebe has included other birds' feathers in the nest construction, a habit she persists in. "Sometimes death is caused by these parasites," writes Green, "especially — which occasionally happens — if a second brood is raised in the same nest." Unfortunately, this story ended like the one a year earlier. The mother seemed to have abandoned the nest shortly after I saw the eggs, and when I took another look, they were gone — the evil work of something besides parasites, I dare say.

Nevertheless, I had been duly warned, so I removed that nest over the winter. I broke it apart to study it and found no feathers, but I still felt that this spring's pair would be better off with a fresh start. Then I started reading about the phoebe's "strong site-attachment." Audubon, in fact, became history's first bird-bander when he tied silver thread to the legs of nestling phoebes and then documented their return over successive years. Today's ornithologists agree that

12

site is all-important for phoebes and that "site fidelity" appears to be a strong instinct in both males and females, such that the same pair will return to the same site for several years in a row. At the same time, I noticed nothing in the current literature about parasite infestation.

They returned right on schedule this year, singing their hoarse song bright and early in mid-February, using the porch rail for their sallying-forth perch. But where is their nest? I can't find it anywhere. I can't help thinking that by removing their old one (both old ones, actually, the one in the front having been long since knocked down by a porch cleanup), I have dampened their enthusiasm for making use of my house.

That would be such a shame—for all kinds of reasons. First, of course, I would love to finally see a brood of phoebes grow up and leave the nest. But if I watched carefully, whatever I saw would be interesting. For example, the phoebe is a so-called acceptor species, meaning that it doesn't put up much of a fight against the dreaded intrusion of the cowbird. Unbelievably, depending on the geographical region, up to a quarter of phoebe nests are parasitized by the infamous interloper. I've had a pair of cowbirds hanging around this spring, and we know she's got to drop her eggs somewhere. Wouldn't that be an interesting thing to see—a big, brown-speckled cowbird egg squatting on top of those immaculate, jelly-bean-sized phoebe eggs. And then what? Play the hero's part and feed the cowbird egg to the dogs? Or witness the bizarre process of the Baby Huey cowbird being reared by the dainty little flycatcher? (I'd have to be a model of stoic objectivity to opt for the latter. In most of these cases, only the cowbird egg will hatch, and even if a phoebe egg hatches a day or two later, the baby is likely to starve.) The good news is that occasionally the phoebe will employ the defensive stratagem of the yellow warbler and build another layer of nest over the cowbird egg—and wouldn't *that* be interesting to see?

But scientific investigation aside, don't we especially love the birds that seem so eager to accept our hospitality, to make our house their home, to come up close and allow us a little intimacy? H. H. Brimley wrote to Bent that he was on a deer stand in North Carolina on a late November day so unseasonably warm that mosquitoes were still "lethargically buzzing about." Out of nowhere a phoebe lit on the end of his gun barrel, then used that perch to pick mosquitoes from his hands and sleeves. The next moment, to better get at the mosquitoes swarming around his face, the bird shifted its perch to the top of his hunting cap. Finally the sharp pinpricks of the phoebe's bill on his face became more than Brimley could bear, so he shooed the bird off—or tried to. It was as single-minded at its feed as a pig at the trough.

The unsentimental truth, of course, is that phoebes are simply indifferent to our presence, as they clearly demonstrate by abandoning us shortly after the end of the breeding season. They're not migrating back south yet; they're as late to leave their summer territory as they are early to arrive. But having gotten from us what they needed for family purposes (a flat, dry, reasonably safe nest site), they head back to the woods. In fact, phoebes are loners, almost never to be seen socializing with other members of their tribe—or even with their own mate except during the brief nesting season.

All of which lends a sweet, sad timbre to its harsh little cry.

Phoebe was all it had to say,
Harrying old winter out the door;
Gone again by the middle of May—
Dude, how 'bout an encore.

Rose-Breasted Grosbeak

Pheucticus ludovicianus

Here's one of those birds that we southern enthusiasts are not likely to get to know as intimately as we might like, and what a beauty it is. That "rose breast" is such an eyepopper that the scientific name (from the Greek *phycticos*) suggests that it must have been "painted with cosmetics."

But that's just for starters. In addition to his gorgeous plumage, the male is reputed to have one of the sweetest songs around—like a robin that has taken voice lessons, as some have said. Bent describes it as "a long phrase with a well-defined form like a pretty little poem, sung in the softest of tones full of delicacy and charm, a voice of syrupy sweetness like no other bird."

What's more, the male is one of the very few birds that not only takes his turn incubating the pair's eggs, but he sings while he's doing it. Edward Howe Forbush says that the first time he ever saw a rose-breasted grosbeak, this behavior fooled him into thinking the male he saw on the nest had to be the female (a strikingly different-looking bird, as he was to learn). Later, having been disabused, Forbush was watching a male on a nest when a hawk flew overhead: "He continued to sing, but so reduced the volume of the song that it seemed to come from far away, raising his voice again when the hawk had passed on." Such ventriloquizing, he found, was another habit of the male.

The pair's courtship activity is also worth watching—especially the way the female turns her head up toward her mate as if to be kissed, and then their bills gently touch. It is "a picture of affection and contentment," we read in *Life Histories*, "quiet and staid with none of the abandon of the farmyard." Plus, the male is a devoted father that not only helps feed the young in the nest but takes over their care after they have fledged. In one instance, when a blue jay absconded with one of the two already hatched young along with the final egg, the female threw up her hands (so to speak) and deserted.

But the male took on the role of single parent with rare determination. He broke up worms into bite-sized pieces; he removed excreta from the nest; he spent the night. After three weeks, when the young bird had just fledged and all the hard work was done, the mother returned to duty.

Not surprisingly, this bird was a great favorite of Audubon's, and not merely because of its outward perfections. He tells of wounding one in the foot, taking it home, and, with no cage handy, giving it the run of his study. After a day of recuperation (on a diet of bread dipped in milk), the bird settled in and began to examine its injured foot, "which," Audubon writes, "was much swollen and quite black." The bird began to bite at its leg above the wound "and soon succeeded it cutting it quite across." The wound healed in a few days, and the bird adapted to its footless leg so successfully that, says Audubon, "it required indeed some care to observe that the patient had been injured." Apparently the bird found Audubon's solicitude to its liking. "It was a lively and very gentle companion of my study for nearly three years."

But, as I say, these stories come to our part of the world secondhand. Although a skinny arm of its breeding range reaches down through the mountains of western Virginia, western North Carolina, and eastern Tennessee, we in the South are not likely to discover the nest of the rose-breasted grosbeak or to hear its lovely song. If we're lucky, though, we can catch a glimpse of this beautiful bird.

DEDE AND RUTHIE AND I moved into these woods on April 1, 1995. We needed to settle in before inviting guests, so a month or two passed before I got a bird feeder up. Consequently, it wasn't until the next April, in 1996, that I looked out the bay window of our little dining alcove, across ten feet of back deck, and straight into the bright scarlet bib of a rose-breasted grosbeak. I about choked on my cornflakes. I knew what it was—after all, it's one of Peterson's cover birds—but

Rose-Breasted Grosbeak (John James Audubon, The Birds of America, vols. 1–4, Special Collections, University Library System, University of Pittsburgh)

I had never seen one in the wild. My, what a sight . . . so vividly black and white, with that astounding red breast. There he was, a male in full splendor, stuffing himself on sunflower seeds and generally looking like he owned the place.

They stayed for two weeks. At least, that's how I thought of it at the time. Sometimes I would see a male and a female, sometimes three birds, sometimes four. Then they were gone. Common sense tells me now that none of them *stayed* at all, but, rather, that for these two weeks—end of April, first of May—the rose-breasted grosbeaks were passing through, and I happened to be lucky enough to live along their migratory flight path.

It was a remarkably dependable occurrence. I might have set my calendar by it. *Oh, here they come. Must be the last week of April.* I also felt as though I were in on a fabulous secret. Being able to predict, and then witness, the arrival of these beautiful birds was profoundly gratifying.

Then in 2001 they didn't come. That was odd, troubling. I could hope that bad weather altered their course, but surely they would have encountered bad weather lots of times. What had happened?

Scientists say that the Tertiary period, from 70 million to 10 million years ago, saw the emergence of most "modern bird families," but let's assume that the rose-breasted grosbeak developed during the major evolutionary explosion of the past few million years, which gave rise to some 8,600 individual species.

We know also that this bird, along with most of our North American songbirds, belongs to the Nearctic-Neotropical migratory system, but, in terms of the particular route it might take, this doesn't tell us a whole lot. Neither does Peterson's map, which shows that the rose-breasted grosbeak has a huge summer breeding range, pretty much all over the northeastern quadrant of the continental United States, and that it might spend its winters anywhere from the West Indies to Mexico to Peru. But let's imagine a small colony whose winter residence is, say, the citrus groves of Cuba's central region, where they fatten on bugs and buds and wait for the mysterious signal—a subtle change in temperature? an angle of sunlight?—that tells them it's time to leave.

Up they rise over the Straits of Florida, over the Gulf of Mexico along Florida's west coast. They're flying at night, like most migrating songbirds, maybe navigating by the stars. Their route takes them through Tampa, and they spend the daylight hours resting and refueling. Food is already plentiful there in late April: bugs everywhere. Another night or two in the sky brings them to the panhandle, to the pretty coastal village of St. Elizabeth, where they rest again. They don't have too much farther to go before they reach their summer home, maybe in the beautiful mountains of northeastern Tennessee, but they have one more stop to make: my forty-acre wood in northwestern Georgia.

Here's the question: How long have they been stopping here, in these deep deciduous woodlands, among these lovely beech, maple, oak, and poplar trees in the foothills of the Appalachians? Or, I should say, how long *had* they been stopping here until 2001? Millions of years? Well, let's be cautious. Let's assume this has been their migratory route only since the most recent ice sheet withdrew from North America, probably some 10,000 years ago.

You probably see what I'm driving at. What had we human beings done *now*? What had we done to disrupt a ritual more ancient than our own history in North America? My mind gnawed on this question. Okay, a few months earlier we had elected George Bush, and, for sure, he wasn't likely to be a friend of conservationists. But, much as I might have liked to, I couldn't connect the absence of my grosbeaks to the election of the president. What was it then? I found the answer in a three-part *Atlanta Journal-Constitution* series, "Georgia's Disappearing Songbirds" by Charles Seabrook. Cell towers. Seabrook reported that cell towers (or, more generally, communications towers) were causing the deaths of as many as 40 million birds a year, most of them nighttime migrating songbirds like the rose-breasted grosbeak. Georgia, at the time of the article's publication, had more than 2,000 such towers, one of the highest per-square-mile densities in the nation, and more were being built all the time. That was it. If new cell towers hadn't killed my grosbeaks outright, their disorienting lights had at least forced a change in the birds' migratory pattern. I would never see them again.

They didn't show up in 2002. Ditto 2003. When I saw a sign on a neighbor's pasture fence saying he had land available for lease to anybody who wanted to build a cell tower, I looked around for an ecoterrorist group to join.

Then, in the fall of 2004, a couple of birds came through, heading south for the winter. Males, but mottled, probably youngsters that had fledged that summer and hadn't gone through their adult molt yet. Their parents hadn't been here in the spring, but they were here now. Reestablishing the old route? That would be cool. On April 26, 2005, a pair of rose-breasted grosbeaks perched gaudily in the new-leaved cherry tree. Right on schedule. A few mornings later, three males and a female were taking turns at the feeders.

As I sit here on a sunny morning at the end of April 2006, watching my small band of rose-breasted grosbeaks in the company of a pair of cardinals, innumerable bright-yellow goldfinches, and a solitary, flighty indigo bunting, I confess that I'm not thinking too hard about cell towers. I'm thinking about the beauty and resilience and infinite variety of life on our lovely planet.

Just don't get me started on George Bush.

Eastern Bluebird

Sialia sialis

> *There must be something wrong with the man who, hearing this*
> *brave and happy bird and seeing him fluttering and warbling in*
> *his lovely vernal dress, does not feel a responsive thrill.*
> —Edward Howe Forbush

> *Dull indeed would be the man that did not feel the thrill awakened*
> *by the first glimpse of brilliant color in the orchard and the cheery*
> *warbling notes borne to our ears on the first gentle breath of spring.*
> —Arthur Cleveland Bent

> *Damn! That's a pretty little bird.*
> —John Yow

The ones headed farther north come through early, as early as February 12 one recent winter. I looked out my bedroom window and there he was, perched in a low branch of our leafless katsura tree—perfect blue above, russet chest, and white belly below—eyes alert for movement in the thawing ground. A week later, out my upstairs office window, I saw two, both males, one in the cherry tree (but never at the feeder) and the other splashing happily in the birdbath. On March 1, we had a flurry of snow and a fire in the fireplace, but if *sialia sialis* says spring is here, who am I to argue? (The oddly redundant Latin name, by the way, reminds me of the day my father drove me off to college many years ago. We were passing through South Carolina, I think, and saw an expressway exit sign for a place called Townville. "Must've run out of names," my father commented. *Sialis* means "a kind of bird.")

According to *The Folklore of Birds*, these beautiful natives of North America have always been a favorite of the continent's original inhabitants. The Navajo see them as heralds of the rising sun and believe that two bluebirds stand at the door of the house of the creator. The Pima of southern Arizona have a story about how the bluebird became blue: One day a flock of these birds found a beautiful blue lake,

high up in the mountains, with neither inlet nor outlet. They bathed in it for four days, and when they emerged, they had no feathers. Four mornings later, their feathers had grown back the brilliant blue color of the lake.

Like so much of the flora and fauna of America, though, the bluebird has suffered from the arrival of "the white man" on these shores. It hasn't been a case of purposeful destruction, of course — everybody loves the bluebird. The story is repeated in a number of sources; call it a case of Anglophilia run amok. It seems that in the late 1800s, the American Acclimatization Society, a group of New Yorkers particularly devoted to Shakespeare and led by one Eugene Schieffelin, set out to introduce into the New World every bird species mentioned in the Bard's works. Unfortunately for the eastern bluebird and other native species, the group's eager researchers turned up the following lines in *Henry IV, Part 1*, wherein Hotspur describes how he will persuade Henry to free Mortimer from prison:

I will find him when he lies asleep,
And in his ear I'll holla "Mortimer!"
Nay, I'll have a starling shall be taught to speak
Nothing but "Mortimer," and give it him. . . .

Following its master plan, Schieffelin's society released a crate of sixty European (or common) starlings in Central Park in 1890. The birds liked their new home. By the turn of the century, they had expanded beyond the city, and by 1925 they covered the eastern United States and Canada. Fifteen years later they had made it all the way to the Pacific coast. Their expansion was no doubt facilitated by their habit of stealing other birds' nest holes, rather than stopping to build their own, and wildlife experts agree that the starlings' piratical habits have exacted a heavy toll on the eastern bluebird especially.

Life Histories offers a graphic account of how the starling operates:

Eastern Bluebird (John James Audubon, The Birds of America, vols. 1–4, Special Collections, University Library System, University of Pittsburgh)

Dr. Musselman once found in one of his boxes a filthy nest, with four half-grown bluebirds cuddled in the bottom; and above them was a two-thirds-grown starling sitting complacently on the smaller birds; "the droppings of the larger bird had soiled and in one case almost covered the head of one of the tiny birds below; one eye was entirely covered and there was a stench which is unusual about such a nest." He destroyed the young starling, washed the young bluebirds, rebuilt a clean nest and returned the young bluebirds to it; the mother bluebird accepted the change and raised her young successfully.

As this story implies, and as all bluebird enthusiasts know, these birds don't excavate. They need to find existing cavities to build their nests, so a ready-made box has considerable appeal. In fact, the untold thousands of bluebird boxes erected by helpful, or hopeful, human beings have at least in part offset the losses inflicted by starlings and other interlopers. If you want to try it, just make sure that your entrance hole is not more than 1½ inches in diameter. Even a quarter-inch bigger, and the nest scavengers will be able to squeeze through.

From my own experience, though, that's not quite all there is to it. Two winters ago I put up the standard bluebird box and sat back to enjoy the show. I was rewarded in early March when a gorgeous male suddenly appeared on top of it, just blazing there in the morning sun. He went in and came out, then flew off. He returned a half-hour later and explored again. When he left this time, I knew he was going to fetch his mate, and I felt like it was my own marriage proposal that was being accepted. But he never returned, and the box, like my poor heart, stayed empty all summer.

What else there is to it is location. I had nailed the box to a tree at the edge of the woods, and of course that was the problem. These insect-eaters feed mostly off the ground and like to be able to scan an open area in all directions from their perch—which no doubt explains why you typically see a bluebird box sitting on its own post out in the open. So this past winter, instead of half-assing the job, I put my box on a sturdy stake and stuck it in the ground in the cleared area beyond the cherry tree.

The male showed up on March 19 in the early afternoon. He checked out this accommodation for a few seconds, then flew off. But he came back again later in the afternoon and spent a little more time. He may well have been searching out other potential sites in the meantime; it's his job to line up a number of possibilities, then get out of the way and let his mate make her choice. So where was she? Three days passed. Had she found a nicer neighborhood? No — there she was on the twenty-third, with a single weed stem in her bill. And then again, a few minutes later, with a bill full — weed stems, pine straw, even a big brown oak leaf — and she managed to push all of it through the little entry hole and into the box. Hurray! Nest-building in earnest.

Since it's a job the survival of the species depends on, no wonder the female undertakes it alone — and takes her own sweet time at it. The authorities say she'll typically spend five days on the project, and *Life Histories* reports that one female made 289 trips to the box with nesting material in her beak. I wasn't maniacal enough to try to count the trips, but I do know that my bird was still building on the twenty-ninth, seven days after she had started. The male, true to his nature, was not helping, though sometimes I'd see him hanging on to the outside of the box, inadvertently preventing her entry. As an unwelcome sign that the job was completed at last, the very next day a female cowbird lit on top of the box and took a long look inside.

Two weeks later, when I couldn't stand it anymore, I shooed the mother off the nest and peered in at those pretty pale-blue eggs. My angle of vision was poor, so I couldn't tell if she had produced the typical clutch of five, but she had at least produced some. I was also reasonably certain that there was no unsightly cowbird egg among them. Over the next couple of weeks she sat tight — well, except for the considerable amount of time she spent sticking her head out the entry hole, as though to keep up with what was going on in the world — while the male did an apparently satisfactory job of keeping her fed.

On the first of May I saw two tiny chicks, and both parents set about decimating the local insect population in a frenetic commitment to child-rearing. Occasionally, and oddly, I would sometimes see the female carrying food back out of the nest—some kind of white food. My binoculars, and a little common sense, corrected me. She was keeping the nest clean by removing her babies' excrement. This, I have to report to the shame of my gender, was a job the male utterly disdained.

On a Sunday in mid-May the youngsters' heads appeared at the entry hole; the father restlessly perched on a limb of the oak tree nearby. Suddenly one of the young pushed through and with frantically beating wings scrambled to the top of the box. I was stunned by how close to fully grown it seemed. It flapped and stretched upward as if to rise, but settled back down. Its father did exactly likewise, the very picture of anxious parenthood. The young one tried again, and this time it tumbled off the box, flapped madly to right itself, and somehow flew to join its father on the branch. It teetered after the clumsy landing, but a couple of wing-flaps helped it settle. Its sibling, obviously unnerved by the commotion, retreated inside the box.

On Monday the nest was empty, parents and children having vacated the premises. I had to congratulate myself on a job well done, but the bluebirds were not ready to do the same. In fact, while the father was coaxing his young from the box, the mother might very well have been building a new nest in preparation for a second brood. What's more, her efforts to do so were quite possibly being impeded by a different—but equally inept—mate.

The truth is that the bluebird cannot count fidelity among its innumerable charms. While mom no. 1 has set about homemaking with dad no. 2, dad no. 1—once he has seen the children safely take wing—will in all likelihood be seeking out a nest site to meet the approval of mom no. 2. And then there's this somewhat lascivious anecdote from E. B. White's essay "Mr. Forbush's Friends": "Male bluebird became infatuated with caged canary. Began flirtation on May 16th, continued it while own mate was busy incubating eggs. Frequently alighted on canary's cage, offered worms, caterpillars. July 1st, saw error of its ways or tired of color yellow, returned to mate, resumed parental duties."

I'll offer no word of reproach. When frigid February gives way to the first mild breeze of March and the lovely bird returns again, let's be grateful for every bluebird hormone we can get.

Belted Kingfisher
Megaceryle alcyon

If you've ever enjoyed "halcyon days," you have kingfishers to thank — at least indirectly. The ancient Greeks believed that these fisher-birds nested on the open sea and so named them *halkyons*, from *hals* (sea) and *kyon* (conceiving). They also believed that the gods smiled upon these birds by calming the waters at their nesting time, the two weeks preceding the winter solstice, and there we have the origin for our term describing days of peace and well-being. The rest of the story is that Halcyone (or Alcyone, as in the bird's Latin name), one of the Pleiades, threw herself into the sea in grief when her husband Ceyx, son of Hesperus, died in a shipwreck, and, taking pity, the gods changed them both into kingfishers.

Now, the belted kingfisher is a striking bird, and fascinating, one whose peculiarity begins with its common name. In an instance perhaps unique in all of birddom, the "belt" the name refers to — the rusty band across the white chest — is worn exclusively by the female. (Audubon, for one, had a problem with this and was all in favor of a name change.) Female or male, though, this bird is distinctive, and anybody who's seen one flying from one end of a farm pond to the other, or up and down its staked-out length of stream or river, chattering like a maniac the whole way, is bound to be impressed. The bird looks like a tough customer, too, with its wild crest, big head, and monster bill. The white scarf it wears around its throat might on another bird be a touch of elegance, but the kingfisher is not elegant — nor, to my mind, particularly godlike. As a matter of fact, if I had my druthers, I don't think I'd want to be changed into a kingfisher. A sweet-singing nightingale, maybe, like Athenian princess Philomela. But a kingfisher? . . .

In the first place, consider the tiny pink feet practically hidden below the massive upper parts. Weren't the Greeks big on *propor-*

tion? In any case, these undersized appendages are pretty much use-less when it comes to grabbing, holding, or transporting prey, which makes hunting and feeding an interesting affair. Not that the king-fisher is inept, by any means. It can fish either from its accustomed perch or from the air during its frequent border patrols, and if on wing, it has the rare ability to hover while it inspects the water below. In either case, once the kingfisher sights its prey, it makes its arrow-like, spiraling dive, headfirst, into the water. Its prey is usually at the surface, but even if the bird has to submerge itself completely, it al-most always comes up with its prize and, carrying it in its bill, returns to its perch.

Here's where strong feet would come in handy (if I may mix meta-phoric body parts). A raptor, for instance, would hold the fish down in its talons and have at it. But the kingfisher is all mouth. If the fish is small enough, he juggles it until he has it headfirst—so the fins won't catch—and swallows it right down. If the catch is larger, in Forbush's memorable language, "he takes it to a branch, post or rock and beats it vigorously, holding it first by one end and then by the other, until it has been reduced to a tractable condition. . . . If the fish is a little too large to be swallowed easily, the bird is compelled to assume a rather strained, uncomfortable position until the extremely rapid process of digestion enables him to engorge and dispose of that part of his meal which at first protrudes from his beak." A little while later, like an owl, he'll cough up a pellet of the indigestible scales and bones.

Then there's the kingfisher's nesting routine. Actually, if the king-fisher nested on the open sea, as legend had it, I guess I could under-stand the gods' affinity for the bird. That's a right poetic notion, after all. But the kingfisher doesn't nest on the sea, or in the trees either. This bird is a cave-dweller, a troglodyte, for goodness sakes, that digs a long tunnel for nesting purposes into the bank of whatever water-way it lives along.

A kingfisher has claimed territory along my stretch of Pumpkin-vine Creek, a broad stream with suitably deep-cut banks on either side, but I'm not hopeful of being able to witness this feat of engi-neering. Because they're often shot at by fishermen who don't want to share, kingfishers are wary birds that prefer to keep their distance. According to the experts, though, the mated pair choose their site carefully, high up on the bank's face to minimize danger from either floodwater or predation, then both birds set about the excavation. One bird works for a few minutes, digging with its bill and scraping the loosened earth backward with its little feet; then the other, which has been waiting nearby, takes a turn. *Life Histories* offers a detailed account of the teamwork: "One would go in and work for two or three minutes and then push the dirt ahead of it to the entrance and fly out over it. No dirt ever came out with the bird that had been digging, but when the other went in there was a veritable fountain spurting out for nearly a minute after it entered. Then this subsided and more digging was done by the bird that had cleared the hole. They kept very close to their schedule of two or three minutes each."

The remarkable fruit of this labor is a tunnel sometimes a dozen or more feet long, with a domed nesting chamber at the end about a foot in diameter and six inches high. (Bent speculates that the really long ones are those that have been used several years in succession, with a new chamber added each year.)

Impressive, yes, but a cave is a cave — dark, dank, and probably fetid, hardly a treetop aerie befitting offspring of the gods. Jim Flegg, in *Birdlife*, holds up the kingfisher as one of those birds whose lifestyle is conducive to "messier conditions than most." He pictures the bird "waddling up its tunnel to a nest chamber lined with foul-smelling remnants of fish and the excrement of its young" and necessarily "soiling its spectacularly colourful plumage," which is why, upon emerging, it "commonly plops immediately down into the stream, splashing vigorously to clean itself."

Flegg's account of the kingfisher's messy domicile is what we might call informed guesswork. The truth, for which we can thank Michael Hamas's report in *The Birds of North America Online*, is beyond Flegg's (or anybody else's) imagining. All of us who've had children understand the poop problem. It's there; the child can't be left to wallow in it; it has to be disposed of. Birds are no different, and, like people, they've devised a variety of remedies, virtually all of which leave the job to the parents. Not so the kingfisher. Here's the deal: The stuff is liquid, not confined to a sac (which the parent might easily pick up and remove), so when nature calls, the nestling shuffles backward, raises its butt, and squirts the feces against the wall of the nest chamber. Then it turns around and uses its bill to hammer loose the earth above the area where the feces were sprayed, which at the same time enlarges the chamber and buries the thin layer of excreta. Whoa.

While we're still spelunking, we notice another interesting thing about the kingfisher young: Their feathers are initially encased in quill-like sheaths, so that for a couple of weeks they resemble baby porcupines. Only when the young birds are almost completely grown, at the end of perhaps three weeks, do the sheaths begin to pop open into juvenile plumage. As Bent puts it, "The transformation from quills to fluffy feathers takes place in a few hours." Hmmm. A hint of sacred mysteries?

Shortly thereafter, it's time for the young to leave their cavern and begin to make their way in the world. *Life Histories* describes them at this point as a "somber-looking lot," sitting tamely about the wharfs or venturing out on short, erratic flights, and looking as though they had not yet got used to the light. Their problem, of course, is that they haven't yet learned to be "fisher-kings."

According to correspondent Floyd Bralliar's detailed account, it's a painstaking process, and one that tests the ingenuity of the mother, whose job it is to pass along this knowledge. It begins with demonstration, as the mother takes her young with her to her perch, and together they scan the water below. When a fish appears, she dives down for the catch and brings it back to the tree limb. With the young presumably salivating, she beats the fish "into partial insensibility," then drops it back into the water. The young cry pathetically at this loss, but the mother won't give in. Finally, the hungriest or most courageous of the fledglings makes a dive for the half-dead fish floundering below. He misses, but clumsily hovers and flutters and keeps at it until he has made the catch, and the lesson takes. Within ten days, any of the young can be seen not only catching his own live fish, but "carrying it to his perch, whacking it over the limb a few times, tossing it in the air, catching it by the head as it [comes] down and swallowing it with as much skill as his mother."

In the final chapter, the children must leave their home, each to establish its own territory by lake or streamside. For the kingfisher is a solitary bird, both males and females defending their own kingdoms until another mating season comes around, when the story begins anew. As the earth greens itself around them, the female alights on the male's perch; he offers her the fish he has just caught. Will she take it?

She does, and after the consummation that follows, the male experiences the apotheosis this essay has been wandering the desert in search of. He soars, according to Hamas's account, then dips close to the surface of the water, then up again into a spiraling ascent followed by a momentary stall and a somersaulting descent. Finally, pulling out of the dive into an ascending glide, he spreads his wings wide open, conspicuously flashing the white on the undersides of his wing feathers. Did Saul of Tarsus witness such a sight?

So what if the digging must now begin again—the long walk through darkness, the descent into the cave, the shadowy underworld? At the end is resurrection and new life. It seems that in puzzling out the kingfisher's link to godhead, we've stumbled across the most ancient archetype of experience—the hero's journey from life through death to rebirth.

It all makes sense now. Except for those little bitty feet.

....

Scarlet Tanager and Summer Tanager
Piranga olivacea and *Piranga rubra*

I'd have to agree with most birdwatchers that, of the two tanagers that summer in my woods, the scarlet is the more striking. With its vermilion body and jet-black wings, it's a fabulous-looking bird. When one deigned to sip from my birdbath on a bright sunny morning this past April, then ascended regally to its normal habitat high in the treetops, my heart lifted with it. Forbush calls it "one of the most gorgeous birds in eastern North America." Burleigh adds that a first glimpse of this bird "cannot fail to evoke admiration difficult to express in ordinary adjectives."

(By the way, *Piranga*, a native name for a South American bird, was co-opted by French naturalist Vieillot to denote this species. Since *rubra*, or "red," was used by Linnaeus to distinguish the summer tanager, *olivacea* ["olive," the color of the female] was used to designate the scarlet. "Tanager," too, comes from South America—specifically from the Tupi Indians, who named these pretty birds *tangaras*.)

Except for its spectacular appearance, however, the scarlet tanager seems little appreciated by the experts. Perhaps because it has no truck with humankind, preferring to conceal itself in the canopy high overhead, humankind has apparently decided to return the favor. Winsor Marrett Tyler, writing for *Life Histories*, observes that "the bird gives us the impression of a placid, indolent, somewhat self-conscious personality, almost lethargic, paying little attention to the life about it." One of his correspondents, Frank Bolles, goes further—goes, in fact, off the deep end: "Mr. and Mrs. Tanager, he in scarlet coat and she in yellow satin, are best measured by contrast with the refined warblers. Their voices are loud, their manners brusque, their house without taste or real comfort. They have no associates, no friends. They never seem at ease, or interested in the misfortunes or joys of those beneath them."

Scarlet Tanager (lower two birds) (John James Audubon, The Birds of America, vols. 1–4, Special Collections, University Library System, University of Pittsburgh)

Excuse me? The fact that a pair or two of these beautiful birds spend the spring and summer in my woods (the very southernmost extent of their breeding range) is clearly a reason for rejoicing, not carping. They sing a lovely song (though to me it's pretty much indistinguishable from that of the summer tanager), and they have an utterly distinct call note (*chick-burr, chick-burr*) that reassures me of their presence even when they hide from sight. They are voracious insect-eaters, dedicated to protecting their leafy domain by devouring the caterpillars that would otherwise defoliate it. And once in a while, maybe when the breeze blows aside the high curtain of green, I do see the gaudy male, dazzling in the sunlight. I'm not sure what more I could ask.

Well, okay, I could be selfish. I could ask that they come a little closer, visit more regularly, get to be neighbors. Which brings me to the pair of summer tanagers, almost equally resplendent, that paid us the rare honor of building their nest in the pear tree not fifteen feet from the front porch. True, the summer tanager, which Bent calls "the southern representative of the family," is a more common resident in the Southeast than the scarlet. It breeds as far south as Florida and is familiar enough during the season to have been given a common name, the summer redbird, to distinguish it from the year-round cardinal. But, still, it's not a bird that the armchair birder is likely to see a lot of. An insect-eater like its cousin, it won't visit your feeder, and until this nest appeared in front of our noses, I considered a summer tanager sighting just as rare and pleasurable as a glimpse of the scarlet. So imagine our surprise. . . .

To be honest, we didn't notice the nest being built. I hate to confess such a thing, but maybe it's not surprising. As is typical, it was far out on a horizontal limb of the pear and well obscured in a thicket of leaves. Not much more than a ragged-looking collection of twigs and stems, it was almost insubstantial enough to see through from below. The fact that it was the work of the female may also have con-

Summer Tanager (John James Audubon, The Birds of America, *vols. 1–4, Special Collections, University Library System, University of Pittsburgh)*

tributed to our failure, since she, pale olive-yellow, is much less conspicuous than the male. (When I later read in *Life Histories* that there was "little data to offer" on the summer tanager's nesting habits — "first, because the birds are far from common and, secondly, because the flimsy inconspicuous nests can be concealed by a single leaf" — I began to realize just how lucky we were.)

Of course, we never saw the eggs either, the nest being an inaccessible (to me) fifteen feet off the ground. But the color picture in Hal Harrison's *Eastern Birds' Nests* shows them to be beautiful — a glossy pale blue-gray, mottled with brown. In fact, they look like a decorative item crafted in fine marble, some Fabergé treasure. What we did see was the mama bird sitting, all through late May and early June. During several days of sometimes violent thunderstorms and driving rain, she hunkered down hard. It was a wonder the nest held. The male never helped with the incubation, but he stayed close by. He gets territorial when his mate is on the nest and chases away any bird that might intrude upon their little sanctuary. When I banged on the bedroom wall to scare off the hairy woodpecker that was tearing up my fascia boards to get at the carpenter bee larvae, the poor guy tried to take refuge in the pear tree. No way. Daddy tanager was on him like a cold rain.

The eggs hatched the second week of June, by which time the mother bird was accustomed to our habit of sitting on the porch in the evening, drinking wine and pitching pistachio shells over the railing. Of course, by this point it was too late for her to do anything about the human nuisance anyway; she and her mate had young to feed.

At first we could see only the three pale orange beaks straining upward for a morsel of food. Well, "straining upward" doesn't quite say it. How about "quivering and writhing in an ecstasy of need"? In a couple of days the chicks' heads were sticking up over the nest rim, odd-looking in their gray down. They were growing fast. We wondered how all three could still fit in the nest.

Both parents fed the young, and it was interesting to watch. We would sit there, all quiet, nothing stirring. Then the three heads would pop up, beaks stretched open, alerted somehow that supper was on the way. Only then would we hear the distinctive call—*picky-tucky-tuck*—and in short order the parents would swoop out of the woods, mama suddenly perched on the side of the nest to feed first.

On a Saturday evening, we had company. Sunday was Father's Day, and we went into the city for the family thing. Monday, the tanagers were gone. Did we miss it? Had they fledged and flown? I read in *The Birds of North America Online* that as early as day 7 after hatching, the nestlings might start to venture out along the branches near the nest, shuffling cautiously and flapping their wings for balance. We hadn't seen any of that, but I figure maybe it's a daytime, rather than an evening, activity. On unsure wings, they leave the nest by day 10 and seek the protection of the surrounding woods. We must have watched them for nine or ten days, so that seems about right. It's also my luck: As soon as we turn our heads, they're gone. What a sudden emptiness in our evening routine.

Only beekeepers say "good riddance" to these lovely, hymenoptera-loving birds. Reporting in *Life Histories*, Floyd Bralliar wrote of a bee-keeping friend whose hive was, inexplicably, not doing well. Sitting down nearby to study the situation, he saw a summer tanager, then another, come to feed, each one taking about twenty bees. When they kept returning, he concluded that there had to be more than two, because no two birds could consume the huge numbers of bees he was losing. He got out his gun and started shooting, and by the end of the day he had killed eight tanagers. Within a few days, "the hive had been restored to vitality"—bringing the story to what I guess we're to consider a happy ending.

But I don't have "beneficial" bees. I have paper wasps, among others, whose chief end in life is to torment the dogs, which twist and flip like dervishes in their effort to snap at the damned things. These wasps, too, the summer tanagers love. Apparently they pick adult wasps out of the air, carry them back to their perch, and beat them to death against the tree branch. They scrape the stinger out and gobble the wasp down. What's more, after killing or chasing away the adults, they tear up the paper nests and devour the larvae. All the more reason to cheer the arrival of these birds as I sit on the front porch, where paper wasps build in the corner of virtually every beam, and to lament their departure.

It was last year that the tanagers came to nest. In late April of this year, I was reading on the porch when I heard the unmistakable *picky-tucky-tuck.* Sure enough, the male flew into the top of the pear tree and perched there ablaze with sexual bravado. He's scouting for a nest site, I practically hollered. They're coming back. Such an amazing circumstance — all the way from Central America, flying by night across the Gulf of Mexico, migrating a thousand miles to set up house in my pear tree.

It didn't happen. Oh, they're in the woods. I see them occasionally and hear them every day. But they've found another tree to nest in. The paper wasps are thriving. The dogs are miserable.

....

Brown-Headed Cowbird

Molothrus ater

Much opprobrium has been heaped upon the poor brown head of the brown-headed cowbird. "This bird is an acknowledged parasite and reprobate," writes Charlotte Green, "with no friends among man or bird." Arthur Bent, glossing the cowbird's scientific name, writes that "the Greek word *Molothros* signifies a vagabond, tramp, or parasite, all of which terms might well be applied to this shiftless vagabond and imposter." Forbush describes the cowbird as "neither polygamous nor polyandrous, just promiscuous."

The invective is occasioned, of course, by the cowbird's "brood parasitism"—that is, the mother bird's habit of laying her eggs in other birds' nests and thus entrusting the survival of the species to the goodwill and hard work of the foster parents.

It's an interesting strategy, isn't it? Many a naturalist has wondered how such a thing could have evolved—or is still evolving. Oliver Austin notes that some species, like the shiny cowbird of South America, still have enough nesting instinct to pick up nest-building material and even to begin construction; they just never finish. It's also theorized that earlier in the evolution of this behavior, cowbirds took over the just-built nests of other species and raised their own young, until eventually the last vestige of parental instinct was lost.

Why? How? Why just the cowbird and not its cousins in the icterid family—the blackbirds and orioles, for example, which are accomplished nest-builders? Assuming, as most experts do, that the cowbird's parasitism is an acquired habit, what in the world happened to its original nest-building ability? Bent gives Otto Widmann credit for an ingenious theory, based on the bird's well-known habit (from which its common name derives) of following grazing herds of buffalo and, later, cattle: "As the pastoral habit of the bird became stronger, it gave rise to the parasitic habit, simply because, in following the roving animals, the bird often strayed from home too far to reach its nest in time for the deposition of the egg, and, being hard

41

Brown-Headed Cowbird (John James Audubon, The Birds of America, *vols. 1–4, Special Collections, University Library System, University of Pittsburgh)*

pressed, had to look about for another bird's nest wherein to lay the egg." As this method of reproduction proved successful, parasitic off-spring became more numerous, and the nesting instinct was more attenuated.

Just as I'm thinking the issue has been sensibly settled, Bent turns the floor over to noted cowbird specialist Herbert Friedman, who writes, "It is somewhat surprising to find a naturalist of Mr. Wid-mann's ability advancing such a theory." The problem for Friedman, it seems, is that "we have no known facts on which to base it, there being no record of a cowbird leaving its nest to follow cattle, horses, or bison."

Another theory (modestly advanced by yours truly) is that the male's courtship display is so clumsy and ridiculous that the female ultimately became unable to contemplate raising a family with such a buffoon. The ritual starts with the male pointing his bill toward the sky, fluffing out his feathers, and burbling his guttural noise. Then he begins the display proper by arching his neck and spreading his wings, raising his tail and bending perilously forward. With all his body feathers fluffed, he spreads his wings the rest of way out, raises his tail the rest of the way up, and . . . topples over. Again and again, until the female has seen enough.

Historically, the cowbird's breeding range has extended southward only to Tennessee, and though it seems to have expanded in recent decades, I despair of seeing this show with my own eyes. But, coincidentally, on a day in late March, three pairs of cowbirds passed through my little aviary. (Only the male has the distinctive brown head, so it was easy to see that I had three males and three females.) They flitted around the cherry tree for a minute, nibbled a couple of sunflower seeds, and then two of the pairs flew away. The remaining female was perched on the limb of an oak tree at the edge of the yard, where the male soon joined her. She flew to another branch and he followed her, at which point I picked up my binoculars. With both birds on the same branch, maybe eighteen inches apart, the male puffed himself out, hunched up his shoulders and spread his wing and tail feathers, then made a little hop in the female's direction. She, in turn, hopped one hop further away. This went on. The female dropped down into the blossoming cherry tree, and the male followed. A fine location for consummation, I thought. But the ritual continued exactly as before, with the male never getting any closer. After fifteen minutes of this frustrating stalemate, the male said to hell with it and went to the feeder. When the female followed, he flew off into the woods.

I can't explain this quasi-display on the part of the male, far as it was from the full show. His not-so-subtle, and even less successful, approach seemed a lot like a kid on his first date, pretending to stretch and then — oops — having his arm somehow drop across the back of his date's seat in the darkened theater. Maybe the bird, like the boy, was a newcomer to the complicated business of courtship.

Since cowbirds continue to exist, we can conclude that copulation does eventually take place, perhaps as the female's only means to persuade the male to desist. But once the deed is done, the birds have no further use for each other. "Contrary to the general practice among the feathered tribes," writes Audubon, "these birds do not pair," and, after mating, "the males seem to regard the females with little interest." Of course, no attachment is necessary, since the cowbirds won't be participating in any of the activities—nest-building, incubating, and feeding and rearing young—that give meaning to the pair bond. "The Cow-pen buntings," as Audubon calls them, "like some unnatural parents of our own race, send out their progeny to be nursed."

So far as the perpetuation of the species is concerned, the female is now on her own. Everybody agrees that she brings remarkable ingenuity to the task, but opinions differ as to the details of her modus operandi. "When the female is about to deposit her eggs," writes Audubon, "she is observed to leave her companions, and perch upon a tree or fence, assuming an appearance of uneasiness. Her object is to observe other birds while engaged in constructing their nests." Having found a suitable target, "she waits for a proper opportunity, drops [her egg], flies off, and returns in exultation to her companions."

That's okay for a general outline of the procedure, but it leaves a few questions unanswered. For instance, is virtually any nest okay, or does the cowbird discriminate? Austin, calling the cowbird the "least selective" among parasitic birds, notes that its eggs have been found in nests of more than 200 other species, which would seem to suggest that the female drops her eggs willy-nilly. Actually, there's a good deal of selection going on. According to Friedman (as cited in *Life Histories*), the cowbird has somehow figured out that four bird families make the best foster parents—flycatchers, finches (including sparrows), vireos, and warblers. More specifically, the five most frequently victimized species are the yellow warbler, the song sparrow, the red-eyed vireo, the chipping sparrow, and the eastern phoebe.

What all the favorite hosts have in common is that they are smaller than the cowbird. Consequently, her egg, larger than the others, will get more heat from incubation and hatch sooner, usually in just ten days. Even when the other chicks come along, the young cowbird's head start will mean that it gets most of the food, to the sometimes fatal detriment of the foster parents' real offspring.

But the cowbird's instinct is not perfect. Occasionally the host's eggs do turn out to be larger than hers, so that her egg doesn't get enough warmth to hatch. Sometimes she happens to pick a species that supplies the wrong kind of food, like the "pigeon milk" of doves. She might even make the mistake of choosing the nest of a precocial bird, in which case the other young will immediately get up and leave, and the young cowbird will be left to starve. Still, says Bent, "the female cowbird is an expert nest hunter." She has reconnoitered sufficiently to find not just one but four or five suitable nests, since her plan is to lay each of her eggs in a different location on successive mornings. Audubon adds that the cowbird "watches its opportunity, and when it finds the nest deserted by its guardians, slips to it like one bent on the accomplishment of some discreditable project." She doesn't tarry, either; the deed is done in less than thirty seconds.

But what if the nest's owner has beat her to it and already started laying? Audubon believes the cowbird is happy for its egg to have the company, because if she chooses a nest "newly finished, and as yet empty, the owners . . . not unfrequently desert it," which would thwart her purpose. But Bent says the cowbird makes a point of laying very early in the morning, "before the host has laid her first egg," and that, in fact, if the host has already begun laying, "the cowbird will remove those eggs and eat them," sometimes leaving just one. Austin offers a third opinion: The cowbird does not eat or otherwise destroy any eggs as she lays her own, "but occasionally returns and removes some, never all, of the host's eggs." Why not all? So that the reproductive instinct of the host is not completely snuffed out. Which explains Bent's observation that the cowbird sometimes leaves one egg uneaten, as well as Audubon's belief that the cowbird really doesn't mind seeing another egg in the nest when she comes to lay.

Imagine the surprise of the young mother-to-be that returns home to find the strange delivery at her door. Audubon's account is characteristically vivid: When the female first makes the disquieting discovery, "she leaves the nest, and perches on a branch near it, returns and retires several times in succession, flies off, calling loudly for her mate, who soon makes his appearance, manifesting great anxiety at the distress of his spouse. They visit the nest together, retire from it, and continue chattering for a considerable time. Nevertheless, the obnoxious egg retains its position."

Well, not always. Robins and catbirds, along with a few other species, won't allow the intrusion and summarily throw the alien egg from the nest. And of the species most often victimized, the yellow warbler has developed her own brilliant defense. If she finds a cowbird's egg in her newly built nest, she buries it under a second layer of nesting material and proceeds to lay her own eggs on top. If the cowbird tries again, the beautiful yellow bird builds again, with the result that the warbler has been known to reside in an "apartment nest" three or four stories high. A few other species, including the scarlet tanager, the American goldfinch, and (as we noted earlier) the phoebe, have also adopted this strategy.

But these are the exceptions. The cowbird is remarkably successful in foisting her young upon her chosen foster family. Or, put another way, the host species are remarkably willing to raise the alien young. A question remains as to just how devastating this parasitism is to the host's own young.

In what Audubon describes as a "remarkable occurrence," once the cowbird egg hatches, the parent birds, "finding a helpless object, for whose subsistence it behooves them to provide," immediately set about the job of feeding it. "The other eggs are thus neglected, and the chicks which they contain necessarily perish." Forbush is equally fatalistic. Because the trespassing cowbird, hatching first, is bigger, reaches higher, and gets most of the food, "the legitimate nestlings remain weak and stunted, and usually either die in the nest or are thrown or crowded out alive by the young Cowbird." He believes that cases where the host's offspring survive are "rare indeed."

Actually, the consequences are not quite that dire. Austin, who noted that the cowbird never disposes of all the host's eggs, asserts that, in general, "some two or three of the host's young will be fledged successfully along with the cowbird." Moreover, Bent reports that a comprehensive experiment with song sparrow nests showed that while unparasitized nests produced an average of 3.4 young, nests that included a cowbird egg successfully produced 2.4 song sparrows. "So the cost of raising the parasite was approximately one song sparrow."

Forbush, for one, would not be mollified. It's simply unnatural, he seems to feel, "to see a young Cowbird tended and fed by a little warbler so much smaller than the great clumsy foundling that in feeding it the little bird seems almost in danger of being swallowed alive." What's more, results of the song sparrow experiment notwithstanding, contemporary ornithologists are worried that a few of the cowbird's tiny hosts whose populations are not robust anyway—like Kirtland's warblers, black-capped vireos, and least Bell's vireos—are indeed threatened by parasitism.

So if you're inclined toward prejudice against the brown-headed reprobate, have at it. But don't forget the story behind the story. The range of the cowbird was once limited to the open grasslands of central North America, where it fed on the insects stirred up by the roaming herds of buffalo. Then came the Europeans, who felled the forests and initiated the devolution of the wild continent into the agricultural and suburban landscapes we have today. Into the new environment the cowbird has expanded steadily, and if it continues to drop its eggs in more nests of more host species, bear in mind that we have invited it to do so.

Red-Bellied Woodpecker
Melanerpes carolinus

Red-Headed Woodpecker
Melanerpes erythrocephalus

The red-bellied woodpecker has every right to complain. Who has ever seen this alleged red belly? From the right angle, and in bright sunlight, I believe that I have discerned the faintest dusting of pale pink on the belly of the male, but I wouldn't swear even to that. Meanwhile, his head glistens brilliant red from crown to nape. In fact, the redbelly is a striking bird all around, with those sharp, black-and-white stripes across its back and, when it flies its swooping flight, nice white patches on its wings and rump. Still, that red head (even on the female, where the red covers only the nape) is the bird's most distinctive feature.

But can it boast? Can it call itself "redheaded"? No. Because here comes haughty *erythrocephalus*, and all pretenders are banished from the court. Not for nothing is the red-headed woodpecker's identity confirmed in its scientific designation (*erythros* meaning "red" in Greek and *cephalus*, of course, meaning "head"). The head of this startlingly beautiful bird is deep scarlet from its neck and shoulders all the way to its crown, the rest of its body a stately contrast of black and white: black back, white breast and belly, white wing patches, and black tail. Few birds are so unforgettable or instantly recognizable, and once you've seen one, you'll understand that the redbelly may have a grievance but, finally, no argument. In this remarkably "monomorphic" species, even the female is brilliantly attired, the two birds together like a king and queen equally resplendent.

Yet the redbelly is an altogether admirable bird, and I welcome it

Red-Bellied Woodpecker (top two birds at right) (John James Audubon, The Birds of America, *vols. 1–4, Special Collections, University Library System, University of Pittsburgh)*

Red-Headed Woodpecker (John James Audubon, The Birds of America, vols. 1–4, Special Collections, University Library System, University of Pittsburgh)

into my yard every season of the year. From late winter, all through the spring, and into the summer I've watched a pair, male and female, take turns at the hanging-dish feeder, clinging with their toes to the rim so that just their heads peer over, like somebody pulling up to the side of a swimming pool or a baby holding itself up by the top rail of its crib. Last spring, oddly, I saw only the female, but I was pleased to be privy to her interesting behavior. When she wasn't at the feeder, she was working away at the base of the cherry tree from which the feeder hangs. A split had developed down where the trunk comes out of the ground, and, since I knew that the redbelly feeds pretty much equally on "meat" (beetles, ants, and grasshoppers) and "vegetables" (seeds, nuts, and fruit), I figured she was trying to vary her diet by picking out whatever insects had taken up residence in there.

The next day I watched a little while longer with my binoculars. It looked like she wasn't taking insects out; it looked like she was picking up the sunflower seeds that had fallen onto the ground and then stuffing them into the fissure at the base of the tree. Or was she picking out insects and then cleaning sap or wood splinters from her bill by pecking at the ground around the tree?

The more I watched, the more convinced I became that she was *storing food* in the tree. It looked like she was hopping around and getting several seeds in her beak — or crop — at one time, then returning to the tree and packing them in. I thought I could see her pause to regurgitate, but I wasn't sure. It also looked like she had enlarged the cavity in the tree to create extra storage space.

Do they do that? I wondered. Yes, they do. As Bent writes, "The red-bellied woodpecker shares with other [woodpecker] species the habit of storing acorns, nuts, insects, and other articles of food for future use." His correspondents have reported seeing redbellies gather up beechnuts and acorns and store them in hiding places (like cracks in fence posts) as far as 300 yards away. Finding them again, I think, would be even more remarkable.

I've since learned that woodpeckers are not the only avian species that makes a habit of storing food. As noted elsewhere, jays — including our familiar blue jay—are similarly provident. Then there are the shrikes, which not only store food but do it much more gruesomely— thence their nickname, "butcher-bird." In *Birdlife*, Flegg mentions the red-backed shrike's habit of "impaling surplus prey" (like frogs, liz- ards, small mammals, and even other birds) on the thorns of a gorse or hawthorn bush—or, adapting to modern times, on barbed-wire fencing—then returning at a later date to finish feeding. Here in America, our northern shrike is similarly bloody-minded—and can- nibalistic. When the supply of insects and mice runs short, this killer picks from a variety of other bird species, dispatches its prey with a few beak-blows to the head, then hangs it in a nearby bush or tree— sometimes suspending it by its head in the crotch of a branch. Once it's secured, says Forbush, the shrike can either devour the meal or preserve it "for future reference."

But you're still wondering: Is the red-headed woodpecker among the other woodpecker species that cache food? The answer is yes, though I can't confirm it from my own observation. I've seen the red- head in my woods; a pair was apparently nesting in the tall stub of a dead pine a couple of years back, and I would hear a harsh *chirr* call as one routinely flew to a further remove whenever I walked up the driveway. But the bird has never been to my feeder or, to my knowl- edge, anywhere near the house. Probably the only reason I had it in my woods even for a while was because I have plenty of beech trees, the source of one of its favorite foods. In general, this bird prefers more sparsely wooded spaces, or trees that border fields, meadows, roadsides, or other open areas, which explains why, these days, I more often see this species on the golf course than in any other locale.

(I doubt that my redbellies were sorry to see their cousins leave. In the winter, especially, the selfish and assertive redhead has a reputa- tion for driving away not only the redbelly and the downy, but also the nuthatches, titmice, and brown creepers—in other words, just about all the birds that, in the redhead's absence, peacefully congregate at the suet and sunflower station.)

But to return to the point, I am assured that the redhead, like the redbelly, enjoys a half-animal, half-vegetable diet and that it, too, stores extra food — especially beechnuts and acorns — for later consumption. However, the feeding habits of the redhead are not as benign as those of the redbelly, as Audubon was the first to note. When the cherries ripen, he observed, the redheads "arrive on all sides, coming from a distance of miles, and seem the while to care little about the satisfaction you might feel in eating some also. Trees of this kind are stripped clean by them." He refuses even to guess at the size of the flocks that descend upon the ripening crop, "but this much I may safely assert, than an hundred have been shot upon a single cherry-tree in one day."

The "animal" half of their diet turns out to be even more objectionable, to the point that we begin to wonder if the redheads' beauty is only feather-deep. Audubon accuses them of sucking the eggs of smaller birds, like bluebirds and martins, and succeeding writers have confirmed this habit. W. G. Smith, reporting in *Life Histories*, describes the redhead as "a veritable butcher" among the nuthatches and chickadees. "And woe to the bird that this villain can reach. It destroys both eggs and young, dragging the latter out of their nests and frequently leaving them dead at the entrance of their holes." Another correspondent watched the redheads wipe out a colony of swallows that had built their mud nests under the eaves of his barn. If the woodpeckers couldn't reach the eggs by sticking their heads in the entrance holes, they tore the nests apart with their bills. Of the dozens of nests the swallows built, according to this account, not a single brood survived.

But back to the positive side of the ledger, the redhead is also an impressive destroyer of insects. A testament to its prowess comes from Bent correspondent E. D. Nauman, who watched for an hour while a female, feeding her young, made five to seven trips per minute "and caught at each trip from one to three or more insects. . . . A computation based upon careful observation showed that a single individual Red-head had destroyed over 600 insects in one hour." Moreover, unlike the redbelly, which prefers to forage for easily accessible foodstuffs, the redhead is adept at probing the trunks of trees for woodborers. Audubon describes how it alights on the side of the tree and at first holds perfectly still, as if listening. If it can't hear or see anything stirring, "the Woodpecker gives a smart rap with its bill, and bending its neck sidewise lays its head close to it, when the least crawling motion of a beetle or even a larva is instantly discovered, and the bird forthwith attacks the tree, removes the bark, and continues to dig until it reaches its prey." (Or, as the legend has it, frightened by the hammer of the woodpecker, "the worm turns" and gives away its presence.)

We might assume from these accounts that the redhead is indiscriminately voracious. But no, not this bird, not the beautiful one — at least not according to *Life Histories*: The redheads "undoubtedly distinguish between colors," reports A. V. Goodpasture, who watched a pair feed throughout the summer; "they find the ruddiest apple and the rosiest peach in the orchard. In like manner, they seem to be attracted by bright-colored insects. They prefer beautiful butterflies, silky moths, and brilliant beetles. The favorite food of this pair was the June-bug; not the plain brown beetle of the northern states, but the beautiful green and gold June-bug of the South."

AS FOR THE PAIR OF REDBELLIES that have been eating my sunflower seeds all spring and summer, I suppose by this point they've also raised a family, but I have no idea where. I haven't seen the nest that she and he have presumably excavated together (since they share all domestic chores), and I guess I'm not likely to. If they needed a dead pine tree, that would be one thing, but apparently, with the exception of the hardest hardwoods, these industrious birds are happy to dig their deep hole in any tree in my woods, deciduous or coniferous.

It would be fun to watch. Bent says it takes them a week or ten days to finish the excavation. Then "they often rest for a week" before getting down to the business of procreation. One of his enterprising researchers managed to investigate a nest he found in a dead cottonwood tree in Mississippi, "a burrow fifteen inches deep with a perfectly circular entrance about forty feet above the ground." I have no idea how the man got up that high, but once he did, he enlarged the hole so he could reach inside and remove the five eggs* he found there. It was late April, obviously a first clutch, and since the redbelly is a "persistent layer," there would be plenty of time for a second or even third. The only question was whether human tampering with the entry hole would discourage a return to this particular nest.

It did not. By mid-May, another clutch of five eggs was in place. But the interesting thing was that the burrow had been deepened several inches, evidently to prevent the extra light caused by the enlarged hole from reaching the floor of the nest. "These birds seem to gauge the depth of their excavations more by the amount of light admitted than from any instinct to dig a certain distance," wrote Charles R. Stockard. "For example, burrows that had their entrance just below a limb or were situated in shady woods were noticed, as a rule, to be shallower than those located in exposed fields or on the sunny side of the tree." I can only suppose that these accomplished architects intuited that the extra light (and heat) would make their eggs incubate too rapidly.

Assuming they are left undisturbed by human or other intruders, the redbelly's eggs are incubated by both parents, the father taking most of the night shift and the mother the day. Their attentiveness is praiseworthy. Neither leaves the nest until the other has appeared to take its place, and both are careful to keep the eggs covered during cooler weather. Brooding and feeding the young are also shared activities—which is a good thing, since, as they grow, the young demand to be fed almost constantly. The work of the devoted pair continues for several weeks after fledging, too; the mother takes some of the young under her wing, and the father takes the others. Redbellies have even been known to bring their young to the backyard feeder,

---

*The eggs of the redbelly, like those of the redhead and most other cavity-nesters, are pure white. The theory is that all birds' eggs used to be white, because the ancestral habit was to cover them or to lay them in covered nests. Since birds developed the habit of open nests, eggs have taken on protective coloration. Though there are many exceptions, it is still generally true that eggs that are still white belong to birds—woodpeckers, owls, and kingfishers—whose nests are still covered, in holes or hollows.

but, much as I would love to, I haven't witnessed this behavior. At long last, like all good parents committed to their children's independence, the redbelly pair shoo the young from the territory.

As for the redheads, I have no intention of impugning their parenting skills. But let's remember what Audubon wrote of these birds: "With the exception of the mocking-bird, I know of no species so gay and frolicksome. Indeed, their whole life is one of pleasure." Maybe it's fair to say that they are better lovers than parents, or merely that they claim a special dispensation. Like the cedar waxwing, they nest late in the season, preferring to spend the springtime playing hide-and-seek on a favorite tree trunk or chasing each other from tree to tree. During these intimacies they form a bond that might last for several years.

Hard labor doesn't suit them. When nesting time finally impends, they would just as soon find a cavity previously hollowed out by another species. If they do build their own, they look for a dead tree or a dead limb of a living tree for easier excavation. A barkless pine stub, like the one they used along my driveway, is a likely choice — not only for its soft wood but for its slick surface. One of this bird's most feared predators is the black rat snake, but snakes of any sort have a tough time holding on to the smooth surface of a dead pine from which the bark has peeled away.

Like the redbellies, the redheads equally share all domestic duties. When one tires of hacking away at the nesting chamber, says Charlotte Green, it calls its mate, which promptly flies home to offer relief. Likewise, both parents incubate, brood, and feed the young. But these parents tire of such responsibilities quickly. While the redbellies might continue to support their young for five or six weeks, the redhead pair have pretty much had it by the end of week 3. By then — who knows? — the cherries might be ripe.

Maybe the pretty bird has heard its praises sung too often. "Beyond question the handsomest of the various species of woodpeckers found in Georgia," says Thomas Burleigh. "The most striking of our woodpeckers," writes Forbush, who adds that the beauty of the redhead inspired the renowned Alexander Wilson to become an ornithologist.

Meanwhile, the dependable, genteel, perhaps somewhat staid redbelly is at this moment clinging to the feeder, taking his one seed and swooping away to the oak tree at the edge of the yard. The chickadees and goldfinches are unperturbed. There's plenty of food, and everybody will get a turn. All is right in my little aviary, and I certainly can't complain.

I have been thinking, though. What if I were to remove my beautifully flowering but nonfruiting Yoshino cherry tree and replace it with a fruit-bearing black cherry? Would their majesties deign to visit?

········

Mourning Dove
Zenaida macroura

I was skeptical when Nicholas Morgan gave me a "squirrel-proof" bird feeder last winter. But *sing halleluiah!* — the thing actually works. When a squirrel puts its weight on the perch rungs, the housing slides down and covers the holes. So the new feeder hangs in the cherry tree, and instead of getting rid of the old one, which had served me well and which many birds seem to prefer, I bought another one like it, along with a double-shepherd's-hook hanging device, and hung them both far enough from the cherry tree so that squirrels couldn't jump into them. (The device also has a "squirrel baffle" that prevents the varmints from climbing up the pole.) Now I have three bird feeders and, much to my amusement and delight, a vast army of frustrated squirrels.

The doves are delighted, too. They're ground feeders, really, and their tiny red feet aren't much good for the kind of vertical perching necessary to get seeds out of a cylindrical feeder; but they don't mind a dish they can perch on the rim of or, better yet, wallow inside of. I was watching one the other day, shortly after I'd refilled the feeders, and it was interesting. The bird moved slowly around and around the center pole that supports the dish, swiping back and forth with its bill to dig down into the seeds. The dove's bill is as weak as its feet, not much good for cracking shells, so I figure it was looking for seeds already out of the shell. Around and around it went, swiping and digging, swiping and digging, and, of course, knocking seeds by the hundreds out of the dish and onto the ground below, where the squirrels were practically standing on their hind feet in anticipation.

Okay. So what? How long can a dove hog the whole feeder like that, anyway. The thing is, though, that what a dove really likes to do after it finishes eating is — in the technical jargon of ornithologists — loaf. Many a time, as a matter of fact, I've looked out the window to

Mourning Dove (John James Audubon, The Birds of America, vols. 1–4, Special Collections, University Library System, University of Pittsburgh)

see a fat dove in each of my dish feeders, settled in as contentedly as a laying hen on her nest. Hell — even the squirrels didn't do that.

But I'm not about to get down on the doves, one of the few species that keep us company all year-round. There they are in the driveway on those early winter mornings when, with the light just breaking, I'm headed up to get the newspaper. I almost run over them in my truck, until they finally take off with their almost musical *whirrrr*. Our dirt and gravel drive always seemed to me to be a pretty silly place to hang out until I realized that they were ingesting their daily dose of grit, which works with their gizzard to grind up their food. Or, in the evening, there they are on the lip of the birdbath, where, unlike virtually all other species, which must raise their heads to swallow their beak full, they plunge their bills into the water and drink their fill.

Best of all by far, even though often unseen on his favorite perch, at the return of spring, the male calls for a mate with his lovely, haunting song: the muffled two-syllable first note followed by the famously mournful *cooo cooo cooo*. I refuse to say exactly how old I was, but I'll confess that I was well grown up before I realized that this distinctive sound was being produced by a nearby dove rather than by a far-off owl. To be precise, it is the call of the unmated male announcing his availability. That other call you've heard, with only one accented syllable — more like *coo-OO-oo* — is likely to be the mated male calling his partner home to the nest.

In fact, no less than their infamous cousins the turtledoves, mourning doves are all about romance. Their courtship is conspicuous from the moment the female approaches the expectant male. He begins with a deep and courtly bow, or maybe several, then straightens up to announce the seriousness of his intent with a loud *cooo*. Soon the couple can be seen "allopreening" (as the experts call it), or (as the rest of us call it) light petting: gentle neck-nibbling and head-pecking. Once the couple begins "billing" (where the female sticks her bill inside the male's and the lovers pump their heads up and down for a few seconds), there's usually no turning back. The pair will be moving in together before you know it.

When they've found the right site — often a horizontal branch in an evergreen tree — the doves begin to build. The actual construction is the female's job, at which she turns out to be inept. The finished product is, by all accounts, absurdly flimsy, a basically flat platform with so little rim that eggs, or even babies, sometimes fall right out. But the funny thing is that the male, whose job it is to haul in all the material, is even less capable. This past March I saw a male perched on top of my shepherd's hook with a bit of dried grass in his bill. He sat for quite a while, twisting his small head this way and that, then finally threw away the nesting material and plopped into the feeder for a bite. Worse yet, W. M. Tyler, writing in *Life Histories*, reports that if the male happens to drop the material he's carrying, he doesn't bother to pick it back up but continues to the nest site with empty bill and then starts all over again. Add the fact that this work takes place only in the morning, and you see why dove nest-building is a relatively long-term project.

What's more, the male appears equally willing, but equally unfocused, when it comes to incubation. The female sits from late afternoon, through the night, until midmorning; then the male takes his midmorning-to-midafternoon shift. But one *Life Histories* observer reported that "the male often left the eggs unguarded for a few minutes about noon while he flew to a near-by watering place to drink."

In fact, Charlotte Green gives the dove low marks in all the responsibilities that romance brings on. "Poor builders, poor housekeepers, and not very good parents," she writes. Their parental instinct is so poorly developed, she continues, "that they readily desert their eggs or young in time of danger."

That seems harsh. In the first place, these romantically inclined birds are, if nothing else, extremely productive parents. Pairs generally raise at least three broods per season with scarcely a day off, much less a real vacation. Maybe they're like the Clampetts in their Beverly Hills mansion, who couldn't figure out the source of that chiming noise but did realize that whenever they heard it, somebody showed up at the door. In any case, the birds' sexual appetite surges as the young of each clutch reach fledging stage, and a new set of two eggs is in the nest pretty much as soon as it's available. This "assembly line" production, as Mirarchi and Baskett put in *The Birds of North America Online*, continues throughout the breeding season.

In the second place, producing all that "pigeon milk" (a cheesy, high-protein secretion of the crop) and feeding by regurgitation can't be easy. Here's a close-up from *Life Histories*: One newborn emerges from beneath the mother and mutely begs for food. The mother responds by opening up and allowing the chick to stick its beak into one corner of her mouth. She then closes tightly and, after a few seconds, begins to pump, her throat muscles convulsing with the effort. The work lasts for about a minute, but no sooner does the first chick withdraw its beak than the other one pushes in. What's more, both have several helpings, with the one not being served constantly trying to wedge its beak into the mother's mouth from the other side. At the fifth feeding, according to this account, both nestlings did succeed in getting their beaks inside the mother's at the same time, one on each side, both presumably competing for the last sip of milk their exhausted mother could produce.

Finally, far from deserting its nest in time of danger, the dove is one of the bird world's many accomplished injury-fakers. "When the adult bird is frightened from the nest by an intruder," writes Forbush, "it may drop to the ground and imitate so well a wing-broken bird as to lead the enemy away." He adds that, in some cases, both parents join in the ruse. As a matter of fact, three distinct forms of this behavior have been documented, depending on the threat level. At Code Red, the dove is perfectly willing to throw itself on the ground right next to the intruder and flutter about as though it were virtually incapacitated.

But certainly the best tribute to the dove's reproductive skills is that its population continues to be abundant. W. M. Tyler suggests that this success is attributable to a survival instinct that tells the bird that it's fine to hang around the barnyard and stable during the nesting season but to get the hell away when hunting season begins in the fall. Actually, the dove's "run-from-the-gun" instinct, if it in fact exists, fails to explain its large population. After all, nearly 70 million doves are killed by hunters every year, which makes the dove a more popular game bird than all the others combined. The thing is, this annual harvest of 10 percent of its population has no effect over the long haul. More amazing still, best estimates are that nonhunting mortality (from weather, predation, accidents, disease, environmental contaminants, and the like) is probably four times greater than that from hunting. And yet, according to *The Birds of North America Online*, all available evidence suggests that the dove's population across North America has increased since the time of European settlement.

Oh, sure, other factors have contributed — especially the advance of agriculture, which turned so much of the continent into a smorgasbord for this grain-seed-loving bird.

But why not face the facts of life? "Birds do it," as the song reminds us, and few birds do it more often, or more enthusiastically, than the mourning dove.

Summer

(overleaf) *Detail view of Whip-Poor-Will* (John James Audubon, The Birds of America, vols. 1–4, Special Collections, University Library System, University of Pittsburgh)

Cedar Waxwing
Bombycilla cedrorum

Except for a couple of scrawny, spindly saplings, my woods are devoid of cedar trees. My cherry tree flowers profusely but bears no fruit, and my nandina bushes must produce the only berries in the world that are not on this bird's diet. Consequently, in our dozen years here in the woods, I have yet to see a single cedar waxwing—that singularly striking bird with its Lone Ranger mask, tawny topknot, cinnamon-brown upper body, buff-to-yellow underside, "waxy" red wingtips (thus its name), and bright yellow band at the tip of its tail.

In fact, my first cedar waxwing sighting was practically my last. I was walking up heart-attack hill toward the library on the University of Georgia campus (this was quite a few years ago) when I noticed a flock of birds devouring the fat orange berries of the pyracantha bushes that provided the building's principal landscape feature. Must've been twenty, thirty, forty of them, buzzing and wheezing and gorging themselves, feasting until the food was gone. I've seen them only rarely since, and, as I say, never once in my own little piece of forest. It seems a shame, but I'm not likely to attract them. Though notorious for their gluttony, they're not seed-eaters, so the backyard feeder doesn't have much allure.

All the more is the pity, because the cedar waxwing is a bird after my own heart. Next to its dashing, cavalier appearance, its love of food would seem to be its most essential characteristic. When Forbush writes, "Cedar Waxwings are such gluttonous birds that they sometimes become so surfeited as to be unable to fly, and have been known to fall helpless on the ground," how can I not remember those Sunday afternoons when I foundered helplessly on the couch after eating my mother-in-law's pot roast and mashed potatoes?

A century earlier, Audubon put it this way: "The appetite of the Cedar-bird is of so extraordinary a nature as to prompt it to devour every fruit or berry that comes in its way. In this manner they gorge themselves to such excess as sometimes to be unable to fly, and suffer themselves to be taken by the hand. Indeed I have seen some which,

67

Cedar Waxwing (John James Audubon, The Birds of America, vols. 1–4, Special Collections, University Library System, University of Pittsburgh)

although wounded and confined in a cage, have eaten of apples until suffocation deprived them of life in the course of a few days. When opened afterwards, they were found to be gorged to the mouth." Dessert, anyone?

Cedar waxwings really love cherries from the orchard, but most of their fruit-centric diet is wild, and the list is long: wild cherries, blackberries, raspberries, mulberries, pokeberries, and cranberries, along with wild berries from the mountain ash, buckthorn, hawthorn, barberry, privet, sassafras, dogwood, nightshade, honeysuckle, mistletoe, black gum, hackberry, holly, camphor, ligustrum, the aforementioned pyracantha, and the eponymous cedar—to name a few.

As an appetizer, the occasional caterpillar or beetle will serve. The cedar waxwing fought a gallant (but losing) battle against the elm-leaf beetle, and its voracious appetite has at times proved beneficial to the gardener. Forbush recalls watching these birds "in a canker-worm year," when the little caterpillars were decimating the leaves of the fruit trees. "Then came the eager birds in flocks and there they stayed, often whispering to one another and always catching worms. Such gourmands they were! They ate until they could eat no more, only to sit about on the branches or play with one another awhile and then eat again." The waxwings cleared out the caterpillars, saved the leaves and, consequently, the fruit, says Forbush, but then the cherries got ripe. "They stayed in the cherry trees with the same persistence that they showed in their work with the canker-worms."

Wait a minute! Wait a minute! Play with one another awhile? Seems a bit anthropocentric, don't you think? Just what kind of "games" do cedar waxwings play to work their appetite back up?

Well, how about "give and take the flower petal"? According to Caroline Stevens, one of Arthur Bent's correspondents, here's how the game is played: One bird, with a petal in its mouth, alights next to his playmate and offers it up. The other bird takes the petal and— here's the important part—hops one hop away. He pauses for a second, then hops back and returns the petal to bird no. 1, who takes it back, hops away, pauses, hops back, and gives it up again. "And so they passed the petal back and forth," writes Stevens, "not three or four times, but twelve and fifteen times, until, tiring of the play, they flew apart."

Makes you hungry just thinking about it, doesn't it?

Another interesting bit of cedar waxwing behavior has given rise to conflicting theories about the bird's nature. This is the well-documented "cherry-passing" routine. A number of writers over the years have described seeing a row of these birds perched side by side on a limb passing a cherry (or berry or insect) from bill to bill up and down the line, over and over again, until it is eventually swallowed by one of the group.

Is this testimony to the cedar waxwing's "sociable" nature, as some writers see it? Is it evidence that the waxwing is "the perfect gentleman of the bird world" and that his habit of "sharing food with his companions" shows "the quality of politeness, almost unselfishness, very rare, almost unheard of, in the animal kingdom"? The scientist, I believe, would consider the waxwing's reputation for gluttony, would notice that every other cherry in the orchard had already been consumed, and would offer a more rational conclusion: These birds are crammed to the crop. The one who finally eats that cherry is the one whose digestive system has worked the fastest.

If it weren't for all this assiduous eating and playing, you could almost accuse the cedar waxwing of being a lazy bird. Forbush implies as much: "All through the spring the Cedar-birds loiter about with nothing on their minds and nothing to do but to eat and grow fat. Many of them even allow early summer to pass before they begin to prepare for family cares." My bias inclines me to take a less judgmental view: The birds are understandably reluctant to rush headlong into the anxieties of marriage and parenthood.

And since the waxwings have waited until the waning of the season, it's no wonder that they prefer to find ready-made nesting materials. If sheep leave nice little tufts of wool stuck on barbed-wire fences, why wrestle with twigs and mosses? Bent correspondent Mary Benson reports that she put out string for the waxwings, hanging it on a clothesline on her back porch, and that after she ran out of string, she began tearing cloth into strips, which they liked even better. "They made no effort to collect twigs or any other nesting material," writes Benson. Well, duh. True, their inclination to steal material out of other birds' nests does seem objectionable, especially when the damage is such that the other birds' eggs fall through to the ground. But who hasn't procrastinated—and then been forced into perhaps regrettable behavior?

So the cedar waxwing loves to eat, play, and dodge its adult responsibilities. The only word I know to describe such behavior is *endearing*. There is one more thing, though. The waxwing appears to have a fondness for alcohol. Forbush, I believe, is the first to tell the story, which was reported to him by a friend who came upon a flock of these birds that were "evidently intoxicated" by the overripe, fermented fruit in a chokecherry tree. "Their actions were very comical, for they were helpless," the man wrote to Forbush. "Some tumbled to the ground where with outspread wings they attempted to run away; still others tottered on the branches with wings continually flapping, as though for balance."

Since Forbush's time, this kind of behavior has become such a staple of waxwing lore that Edgar Reilly, in *The Audubon Illustrated Handbook of American Birds*, scarcely bothers to mention it: "Occasionally gets drunk from eating overripe cherries." Thankfully, Charles Seabrook, writing in his weekly *Atlanta Journal-Constitution* nature column, restores some of the color to this wonderfully odd story: After gobbling up overripe berries, Seabrook writes, waxwings "may become so intoxicated that they fly . . . well, drunkenly, and crash into buildings or pass out on the ground. They can be picked up easily. Cats and other predators may make a meal of them. If you come across intoxicated waxwings, the best help you can render is to guard them from predators while they sleep it off. After a few hours, they will sober up and be on their way."

Shall we make this a cautionary tale? Audubon, in those pre-PETA days of a century and a half ago, reports that cedar waxwings fatten up "and become so tender and juicy as to be sought by every epicure for the table." He tells of a friend who tried to send a "basketful of these little birds" to New Orleans as a Christmas present, but before they could arrive, "the steward of the steamer, in which they were shipped, made pies of them for the benefit of the passengers."

Four and twenty waxwings baked in a pie? Shall we say that such a fate is the proper reward for these pretty, vain libertines who think of nothing but self-indulgence?

Hmmmm. Time for my nap.

American Goldfinch
Carduelis tristis

The very first entry in the journal I've kept since we moved to the woods in the spring of 1995 mentions that my bird feeder had been up for a month and, to that point, the goldfinches were the only birds to have discovered it.

They have kept on discovering it. During the winter months it's all I can do to keep them supplied with sunflower seed. One morning this past February, I counted fifteen at the feeders and on the ground below. (Not that such numbers are likely to impress birders in the Northeast, where goldfinches are reported to gather by the hundreds in anticipation of the breeding season.)

In early April, here in Georgia, the male begins to put on his resplendent dress. By the middle of the month the molt is complete, and I can look out my window and see a half-dozen males bursting in lemon-yellow brilliance among the new green leaves of the cherry tree. At the same time, I begin to hear their cheerful song, typically rendered as a canarylike *per-chik-o-ree* and always, it seems, sung by a choral group. In early June, still watching the handsome males at every feeder, I begin to wonder, and then, two weeks later, I finally see a male and a female feeding together, looking very much like an item. I'm thinking, *Hey, the wrens have already raised two families. What took you guys so long?*

Well, that's just the way it is with *Carduelis tristis*, and the Latin species name hints at why. *Carduelis* derives from *carduus*, meaning "thistle," a plant that supplies both food and nesting material for the goldfinch. Since the female insists on lining her nest with thistle down, she can't build until the plant flowers, which might not be till midsummer. Like the waxwing, writes Forbush, the goldfinch is "late to the nest, seeming to frolic most of the summer long." Which, by the way, makes the individual name, *tristis* (or "sad"), a complete mystery. Linnaeus is said to have applied this term based on the bird's sound, but, as bird-name expert Ernest Choate puts it, "As the call is not mournful it is difficult to understand the reason for Linnaeus' choice."

No, forget sad. This bird is all about gathering rosebuds and *carpe-ing diem*. *Life Histories* includes this account of a goldfinch get-down from naturalist John Burroughs, writing in 1904:

> All the goldfinches of a neighborhood collect together and hold a sort of musical festival. To the number of many dozens they may be seen in some large tree, all singing and calling in the most joyous and vivacious manner. The males sing, and the females chirp and call. . . . The best of feeling seems to pervade the company; there is no sign of quarreling or fighting; "all goes merry as a marriage bell," and the matches seem actually to be made during these musical picnics. . . . I have known the goldfinches to keep up this musical and love-making festival through three consecutive days of a cold northeast rainstorm. Bedraggled, but ardent and happy, the birds were not to be dispersed by wind or weather.

Anybody else having a flashback? Yasgur's farm? August 1969?

Once the thistle and cattail down finally become available, the female applies considerable skill and artistry to building her cozy, cuplike nest. (The male sings merrily at her side, or, if he's anxious, he might pick up some nesting materials to give his mate the idea, which he invariably then drops. In any case, he's no help.) The nests are durable enough to last several years (although the goldfinches seldom return to them) and so tightly woven they're said to hold water. Before the down lining is added, the bird sometimes stitches together the coarser materials, like strips of bark or leaves, with spider or caterpillar silk. In one *Life Histories* account, the female flew into the nest with a spider's cocoon case, with which she circled around and around, putting it down to attach the thread, then picking it up again, unraveling it as she went. "Thus the strands of cobweb were drawn over the surface of the nest and helped to bind together the materials of which it was composed."

Some experts believe that the goldfinch tends to build within a

American Goldfinch (John James Audubon, The Birds of America, vols. 1–4, Special Collections, University Library System, University of Pittsburgh)

hundred yards or so of food sources (like my feeders) and that, since these birds are not particularly territorial, the more food available, the more nests there will be. It's true that the only ones discovered by Georgia ornithologist Thomas Burleigh were high up in short-leaf pines; but other writers claim to have found them low to the ground, so I'm reasonably hopeful of stumbling upon one of these little gems of craftsmanship. It's likely to be cradled in three or four horizontally growing branches, I am told. So, okay, I'm keeping my eyes out.

When it comes to parenthood, the goldfinch's reputation is somewhat spotty. By some accounts, it's as though they've been unable to give up their carefree hedonism. One *Life Histories* correspondent comments on the birds' "peculiar behavior of abandoning many nests before completion, or at times after completion but before egg-laying. Occasionally, nests with eggs, or even with young, are abandoned." Forbush adds that the parents tend to leave the nestlings pretty much to themselves "and never seem to manifest such fussy anxiety about them as is displayed by the Robin or the Catbird, nor are they so assiduous about cleaning the nest."

In the male's defense, though, it must be said that even if he's useless as a nest-builder, he's a hardworking breadwinner. During the two weeks his mate incubates her pale blue eggs, as well as during the few days of brooding, he feeds her faithfully and also supplies the food that she, in turn, feeds to the young. Since they nest so late, goldfinches generally produce only one brood, but if they get started early enough, "experienced breeders" sometimes go for two. In these cases the male really proves his mettle, because he's left in charge of the first brood while the female flies off to find another mate. I'm almost tempted to speculate that the male is the stable partner in the relationship, that it's the female who can't get over those good old days of free love and giddy irresponsibility.

Given its tireless consumption of weed seeds, the goldfinch's entirely vegetarian diet is a boon for humankind but something of a mixed blessing for the birds themselves. On one hand, food is generally plentiful, and the birds are expert gleaners. Forbush describes how two or three together might be seen bending the top of a slender weed to the ground, where they stand upon it and greedily devour the seed-head. On the other hand, some of their favorite foods, like burdock, fatally entangle the tiny birds as they try to extract the seeds. What's more, the all-vegetable diet places the bird in a weird "lose-lose" relationship with the interloping cowbird, which sometimes parasitizes the goldfinch nest. Even if the cowbird egg hatches, the chick's growth is retarded by the low-protein, meat-free diet, and it dies before fledging. At the same time, the parasitism often spells doom for the eggs and young of the goldfinch as well. (On a pleasanter note, the goldfinch is among the clever birds that sometimes thwart the cowbird by burying its egg under a second layer of nest.)

Given the striking beauty of the little "wild canary," it's not surprising that the goldfinch has been a popular cage bird in times past. Audubon says they will "live to a great age" in confinement, but only if they've been raised in captivity or else trapped at the right season: "If it has been in spring that they have lost their liberty," he writes, "and they have thus been deprived of the pleasures anticipated from the previous acquisition of a mate, they linger for a few days and die." Usually no sentimentalist when it comes to killing or trapping birds, Audubon goes soft on the merry, company-loving goldfinch. Describing a captive bird that was trained to draw its water from a glass by hoisting a tiny bucket and to pull "a chariot" of seed toward its bill, he writes that in this "distressing occupation," the bird "was doomed to toil through a life of solitary grief, separated from its companions, wantoning on the wildflowers, and procuring their food in the manner in which nature had taught them."

These days, though, not much threatens the healthy and stable population of this lovely little songbird. Since its breeding range doesn't extend much farther south than my own woods, I feel fortunate to have my little aviary brightened by its presence. At this moment, in fact, in the middle of a hot afternoon in late June, I'm watching a pair, "sitting in a tree, k-i-s-s-i-n-g." Swear to God. They're side by side on a little branch high up in an oak, the male turning his open beak toward the female, and she quickly touching its inside with hers. The thistle hasn't quite flowered yet, but this pair is definitely getting ready.

Sweet birds, you are so welcome here. May your nest thrive. And if at the end of the season you invite a few dozen of your northern cousins to come down for the winter, that'll be fine, too. The feeders will be full.

Wood Thrush

Hylocichla mustelina

Here's another in this book's long list of embarrassing revelations. I've never seen a wood thrush. Heard, yes—a point we'll come back to. But seen? No. I wanted to know how egregious a failing this was, so I conducted a small poll.

I asked noted horticulturist and backyard birder Don Hastings if he'd ever seen a wood thrush. "Sure," he said. "One of Betsy's favorite birds."

"Where do you see them?"

"Scratching in the leaves underneath the Japanese maple."

"You know they look a whole lot like a brown thrasher," I cautioned.

"Yeah, but their tails are shorter."

I asked my brother Richard, whose enthusiasm for all things outdoors far exceeds my own. "Of course," he said.

"You know they look a whole lot like a brown thrasher," I said.

"I'm not an idiot," he said.

I asked novelist, naturalist, and all-around polymath Mary Hood. "I *am* the wood thrush," Mary replied, which I took as a yes.

Well, I've seen pictures, which is how I know it looks a lot like a brown thrasher—except that, in addition to having a shorter tail, it's plumper, has dark spots rather than streaks on its white breast, and lacks the thrasher's wing bars. The thrasher also has yellow eyes, which I have seen, while the thrush's, which I obviously will never see, are dark.

(After belaboring this comparison, I guess I should point out that, actually, the wood thrush and the brown thrasher are not related. The thrasher, along with the mockingbird and catbird, belongs to the family *Mimidae* [the "mimics"], whereas the thrush family name is *Turdidae*. So, then, it's the thrasher whose white-and-dark-patterned breast is the anomaly. All of our so-named thrushes [gray-cheeked, Swainson's, hermit, and wood] have this sort of pattern on their

breast, and even the robin and bluebird announce their *Turdidae* bloodline through the spotted breasts of their adolescent offspring.)

Now, where was I? Oh, pictures. Well, it looks to be a pretty enough bird, with a pretty Latin name: *Hylocichla mustelina*. The first term says it all, combining the Greek *hyle* ("a forest") with *cichla*, or "thrush." *Mustelina*, or "weasel-like," apparently refers to the bird's tawny color. Put it together—*Hylocichla mustelina*—and it's every bit as mellifluous as "Texaco gasoline," which, if I remember, one of Truman Capote's characters thought was the prettiest name in the world.

But nothing, neither pretty pictures nor pretty names, prepares us for this bird's song. From late spring through the middle of summer, the thrush's three flutelike notes—often rendered *ee-o-lay*, but poorly served by any rendering—are the first birdsong we hear in the morning and the last we hear as the woods grow dark at night. Though they have their own ways of expressing it, most bird writers seem to share my opinion that any day so begun and ended can only go so wrong.

Audubon writes that this thrush's song, "although composed of but few notes, is so powerful, distinct, clear, and mellow, that it is impossible for any person to hear it without being struck by the effect which it produces on the mind." He goes on to call it his "greatest favourite" and describes it as a harbinger of day that invariably predicts the parting of the nighttime storm clouds. "For no sooner are its sweet notes heard than the heavens gradually clear."

Reporting from the distant galaxy to which the thrush's song has transported him, Forbush writes that once it settles on its evening perch in the treetops, "unhurried, the thrush pours forth a series of intermittent strains which seem to express in music the sentiment of nature; powerful, rich, metallic, with the vanishing vibratory tones of the bell, they seem like a vocal expression of the mystery of the universe, clothed in a melody so pure and ethereal that the soul still

Wood Thrush (John James Audubon, The Birds of America, vols. 1–4, Special Collections, University Library System, University of Pittsburgh)

bound to its earthly tenement can neither imitate nor describe it."
As we listen, he writes, "we lose the sense of time—it links us with
eternity."

As we might expect, the reproductive urge brings out the best
of the male's abilities. "At the beginning of the season," says Bent,
"the male sings his most beautiful, varied, and complete song from
the tops of the highest trees." One of his correspondents adds that
after the courtship flight and subsequent consummation, the song of
the male is "noticeably loud and long." But as we might also expect
from such an artist, music and sex are about all the male contrib-
utes to the life cycle of the species. The female selects the nest site,
builds the nest, and incubates her eggs without assistance. She also
turns the eggs when necessary, removes the shells when they hatch,
and broods the young with no relief from her mate. The male does
deign to bring food to the nestlings, but even here he must hand it
off to the female, who does the tedious work of removing all the indigestible parts—heads, wings, brittle shells—before passing it on to
the young.

Like those of her cousin the robin, by the way, the thrush's three
or four eggs are quite beautiful—smooth, slightly glossy, and so uni-
formly blue-green that they look like Easter eggs double-dipped in
dye. Their nests are similar, too, even down to an odd peculiarity;
both the robin and the thrush like to include something white in
their construction—paper, cloth, lace, a white flower petal, or maybe
even a white chicken feather.* Writing about the thrush in *Life Histories*, Florence Weaver suggests that, although it might seem that
such an addition would make the nest more conspicuous, it may well
have the opposite effect, acting as a "concealing coloration" in that "it
breaks the nest's contour." She goes on to note that the female may
use the white triangle of her chin and throat for the same purpose.
"It was noted that when something happened to frighten the incu-

*So is the use of white material a nest-building habit common to other members of
the family *Turdidae*? Nope. Harrison makes no mention of such objects in the nests of
the bluebird, the veery, or any of the other birds named thrush. Sorry.

bating bird, she pressed her body more deeply into the nest and held her head back farther, pointing her bill upward. This made the white throat still more conspicuous."

If you're lucky enough to come upon a sitting female — in the low branch of a dogwood tree, where Audubon says to look, or in the fork of a small sapling — she won't scare. Her nesting instinct is so strong that she'll just hunker down, hoping her "concealing coloration" is having its proper effect. But I haven't been so lucky, and you might not be either, since, historically, the wood thrush has preferred to nest in the dim shadows of the deep woods. Some say that this kind of habitat supplies the damp leaf mold that the thrush uses in the foundation of its nest, but another theory is that the bird prefers the forest gloom because its relatively large eyes are sensitive to light. Burleigh, for example, writes, "In common with other thrushes of this genus it seems to dislike direct sunlight, rarely leaving the dense shade of the thickets it inhabits." Most writers agree that it migrates at night for the same reason.

But then, again, you might get lucky, because a contradictory theory is also current — that is, that the bird has been moving to town, where it quickly adopts town ways, not only pulling worms out of suburban lawns but even bathing in the sprinklers. "When living in our towns and cities," writes Bent, "the wood thrush loses much of its natural shyness and timidity. We often see it leave the shelter of the shrubbery or leafy thickets in the more secluded borders of our grounds and come out onto the lawn in search of food, almost as fearless as a robin." Harrison adds that as it becomes more tolerant of people, the wood thrush is increasingly choosing nest sites close to houses as long as there is a wooded area nearby.

So what am I, chopped liver? I've got dogwood trees, I've got shrubs, I've got a yard full of grubs and worms, and I've certainly got plenty of woods. But, no, I'm resigned; I'll never see this bird — even if everybody else in the world does.

Maybe that's okay, though. If this bird's haunting summer song remains, for me, disembodied, doesn't that make it all the more powerful and mysterious? After all, Thoreau never talks about *seeing* the bird, but here is what he does say: "Whenever a man hears it he is young, and Nature is in her spring; wherever he hears it, it is a new world and a free country, and the gates of heaven are not shut against him."

I could do worse.

Yellow-Billed Cuckoo

Coccyzus americanus

After a dozen years here in the woods I still occasionally see birds I've never seen before. A brown creeper showed up, for instance, after I finally got around to hanging a suet feeder, and over the past couple of years I've noticed blue-gray gnatcatchers darting in and out of the pear tree in the front yard. In most of these cases, whether because of their appearance or behavior, I have some inkling of the newcomer's identity.

Not in every case, though. Several years ago I was sitting on the front porch when I saw some motion in the foliage up the driveway a bit. I trained my binoculars on the spot, and within a few seconds the bird moved in such a way as to come into full view. "What in the be-jeezus is that!?" I hollered to the dogs. This was one of the most striking and elegant birds I had ever seen — rich brown upper parts contrasting sharply against the pure white underside; the long, pale, curved bill; and, most distinctive, a pattern of white circles against black on the underside of its extralong tail — and I had no idea what it was.

But there's no mistaking this bird for any other, so a quick thumb through Peterson was enough to identify it with certainty. A cuckoo in my woods! Honestly, as far as I knew, this was a bird that existed entirely in fable and legend. I happened to be reading Jim Flegg's *Birdlife* at the time, and, turning to what he had to say about the cuckoo, I discovered that it, like the cowbird, is a "notorious nest parasite" that lays its eggs in another species' nest and lets the foster parents do the child-rearing. "As an elegant further adaptation to the Cuckoo's already sophisticated mode of parasitism," he continues, "this bird's eggs often hatch in only eleven or twelve days, so giving the young Cuckoo the chance to shoulder its foster parents' own eggs out of the nest before they hatch: an easier, less energy-costly exercise than evicting struggling nestlings."

If we are surprised by the fact that the cowbird nestling is fed by its foster parents no matter how little it resembles their own young, the fledgling cuckoo, says Flegg, is even more remarkable. Leaving

Yellow-Billed Cuckoo (John James Audubon, The Birds of America, vols. 1–4, Special Collections, University Library System, University of Pittsburgh)

the nest, it takes up a position in a bush or on a post nearby, and "with its particularly wheedling cry and rich orange-crimson gape . . . it seems able to stop almost any food-carrying bird in its tracks and draw it, remorselessly, to deposit the food load in the Cuckoo's gaping maw." He cites the case of "one unfortunate Wren," which, perching on a young cuckoo's head and leaning over to push some food into its mouth, actually lost its footing and fell into the fledgling's throat, "in the process suffocating both itself and the Cuckoo."

Whoa. Good stuff. Who knew what kind of weird behavior might be going on right here in my little piece of forest? It wasn't too many days after my original sighting that I saw my yellow-bill again, but this time, very clearly, it was working hard to snap a twig off of a maple tree. This looked a whole lot like nest-building activity to me, so further research was called for.

You're probably already ahead of me. It turns out that Flegg, a Brit, was writing about the common, Old World cuckoo, whose habits are quite different from those of its American cousins. The yellow-bill, I soon learned, does in fact build its own nest and rear its own young, thank you very much, and what it may therefore forfeit in ingenuity it more than makes up for in dignity and decency.

Or so I thought. There turns out to be much more to the story of the yellow-billed cuckoo, surely one of the oddest and most interesting birds ever to set feather in my forty-acre wood.

To begin with, yes, the yellow-bill builds its own nest, but it does a crappy job of it. The thing is so flimsily constructed that you can see the eggs through the bottom, and it's so flat that if you can't see the eggs, it's probably because they've rolled out and shattered on the ground at your feet. "One of the poorest nest builders known to me," writes Major Bendire in *Life Histories*, who notes also that the "shallow, frail platforms" are so small that "the extremities of the bird project on both sides."

Wait. There's more. Sometimes you'll find a yellow-bill nest with, instead of the usual three or four eggs, maybe six or eight. That's because one mating pair has decided not to build after all, and the female has laid her eggs in the nest of another yellow-bill. Ornithologists call this behavior "intraspecific" brood parasitism, and laypeople like me say, well, okay, at least they're related. But—you guessed it—the yellow-bill also *occasionally* indulges in "interspecific" brood parasitism and is on record as laying its eggs in the nests of at least eleven other species, including not only its cousin the black-billed cuckoo but also the robin, the catbird, the cedar waxwing, the cardinal, the wood thrush, and others. Finally, according to Janice Hughes in *The Birds of North America Online*, the yellow-bill even shows evidence of "egg mimicry"; that is, it tends to lay its blue-green eggs in the nests of birds whose eggs are similarly colored.

It's the uncertainty that I find so remarkable. The cowbird and the European cuckoo know what they are going to do; they are going to lay their eggs in other birds' nests. Pretty much every other bird on the planet knows what it is going to do; it is going to build its own nest for its own eggs. But, apparently foundering in some evolutionary eddy, the yellow-bill doesn't know what it is going to do. The poor bird seems, in Matthew Arnold's words, "Caught between two worlds, / One dying, the other powerless to be born."

Now that I think about it, the nest-building activity I saw my yellow-bill engaged in may not have been nest-building after all. These furtive birds have another odd habit, well described by Hughes. When the female is ready for copulation, she signals her mate with a tail-pumping gesture. Taking his cue, the male heads to a nearby tree, snaps off a small twig, flies with it to the female, and lands directly on her back. As they position their bodies for sexual contact, he extends the twig over her shoulder, and both birds hold onto it during their few seconds of consummation. Wow. It's been speculated that the twig may substitute for a food item in the relatively typical male-to-female offering, but the image of the two birds holding onto it together during the sex act strikes me as, in the world of bird behavior, wildly erotic. (Is their uncertainty as to what to do with the twig afterward—sometimes dropping it, sometimes using it as nesting material—a sign of their confusion as to whether to build or not?)

Perhaps paradoxically, the yellow-bill seems in a hurry to get started on its sometimes bizarre journey through life. Or maybe it's just in a hurry to get through its inauspicious first few hours. As Bendire puts it, "The young when first hatched are repulsive, black, and greasy-looking creatures." It doesn't help that—as we saw in the case of the kingfisher—the quills, or feather sheaths, that soon appear make the nestlings look more like porcupines than baby birds. On about day 6, though, a remarkable transformation takes place. An observer for *Life Histories* described it this way: "About ten-thirty in the morning the sheaths began to burst, and with each split a fully formed feather was liberated. This process took place with such rapidity that it reminded me of the commotion in a corn popper or a rapidly blooming flower. All the while I was within three feet of the bird, and could see every new feather, as it blossomed, so to speak." A day later, these birds are ready to go, such that the entire process, from the start of incubation to fledging, takes only seventeen days—a full week quicker than the typical passerine.

How about the diet of this bird? A seed here, an insect there, the occasional wild berry? No. In this, as in everything, the cuckoo asserts its inimitable self. Fortunately for the farmer and the forester, the yellow-bill never saw a caterpillar it didn't love—including such destructive species as tent caterpillars, fall webworms, and gypsy moth caterpillars—all of which it consumes by the thousands. Nor does it discriminate, as most birds do, against hairy or spiny caterpillars, the constant ingestion of which has forced this bird to develop perhaps the rarest of all its rare and wonderful abilities. Forbush explains that "when, in time, the inside of the bird's stomach becomes so felted with a mass of hairs and spines that it obstructs digestion, the bird can shed the entire stomach-lining, meanwhile growing a new one—a process that would be beneficial to some unfeathered bipeds could they compass it."*

---

*Audubon accuses the yellow-bill of eating the eggs or young of smaller birds, and while some later writers doubted this idea, recent research indicates that it's true after all. So an interesting question remains: When, as sometimes happens, the yellow-bill is "mobbed" by smaller birds, is it because they fear the larger bird as a predator or a brood parasite?

What's left? Oh, of course, the yellow-bill's song. Austin tells us that only the common cuckoo of the Old World distinctly says its name. The yellow-bill says much more than that—an utterly distinctive vocalization usually rendered something like *kuk-kuk-kuk-kuk-kuk-keow-keow, keowlp, keowlp,* with the later syllables slower and more drawn out. Audubon calls them "dull and unmusical notes . . . not unlike those of the young Bull-frog." My musical taste is not so refined, and I find the yellow-bill's notes as singular and marvelous as everything else about it. The bird is said to call more frequently when rain is on the way (thus its familiar name, "rain crow"), which perhaps explains why I haven't heard it all this long, dry, hot summer.

Every writer comments on this bird's shy, secretive nature, how it likes to sit motionless and unperturbed, hidden in summer's thick foliage. For me this demeanor makes its odd behavior all the more fascinating—as if this most unusual of birds were reluctant to call attention to itself, as if it preferred to keep its mysteries mysterious.

If this is the yellow-bill's survival strategy, though, the sad truth is that it's not working. According to current statistics, the bird's numbers are declining precipitously throughout its range, most especially in the West. Already the yellow-bill is gone from British Columbia, Washington, Oregon, and possibly Nevada. In California, the destruction of its preferred riparian habitat, combined with pesticide use, has reduced a population that once numbered more than 15,000 pairs to a mere 30.

Maybe this strange and lovely bird needs a new game plan. Maybe it ought to come out of its seclusion, belch out a few of those bullfroggy, unmusical notes, and get itself noticed.

Given the fact that the *people* who took its habitat aren't likely to give it back, the *bird* has got to do something.

....

Chimney Swift
Chaetura pelagica

Such a comfort to see the chimney swifts darting through the air around the house as we sit on the front porch these summer evenings. I'm sure they're doing a lot better job at mosquito control than our citronella candles. And such a pleasure to hear their lovely twittering as they nest and raise their young inside our chimney. When they fly in and out, their wingbeats sound like distant thunder. I've been fooled more than once into thinking maybe a storm was coming to break a summer drought.

(Caveat for the absentminded: If you're lucky enough to have swifts in your chimney, remember to close your flue at the end of winter. We returned home from a short vacation one summer to find the whole swift family dead and scattered around the house — including, most bizarrely, one we found inside the carafe of the coffeemaker.)

These amazing insect gleaners feed on the wing all day long, never once touching down to take a break. Since they're in the air from dawn to dusk anyway, I guess their long-distance migration from Peru and Chile, up through Mexico, and on to North America just seems like puddle-jumping. Their aerodynamic bodies ("cigars with wings") and tiny feet make them so much more at home in the air than on land that, according to most experts, they court, mate, and sometimes even die while in flight. Some would add "cavort" to that list. Admittedly, most of the swift's zigging and zagging is in pursuit of those elusive insects, but Forbush describes these birds as "extremely playful" and attributes at least some of their aerial acrobatics to their "frolicsome spirit." They even stay airborne at the approach of violent weather, he writes, and "seem to enjoy riding the storm."

When it's not in the air, the swift is using its sharp little toenails and stump of a tail to cling vertically to its roost during the night. *Chaetura*, or "bristle-tail," might seem like an odd designation for a bird that seems to have no tail at all, but if you look at a good photograph or illustration, you can see the needlelike bristles sticking out of the end of its seemingly truncated tail feathers. Otherwise, the

Detail view of Chimney Swift (John James Audubon, The Birds of America, *vols. 1–4, Special Collections, University Library System, University of Pittsburgh)*

stumpy tail is an easy way to tell this bird from the equally speedy and acrobatic barn swallow, which has a distinctly forked tail. (I recently had a good look at both tail and feet when a swift flew in through the unscreened window beside my desk. I had inadvertently left the window open at the end of the workday and discovered the swift fluttering to get out another window the next morning. I grabbed it up in a towel to carry it outside, which worked fine until I faced the problem of freeing its toenails—one at a time—from the fluffy terry cloth.)

The diminutive size and weakness of the swift's feet gave rise to one of ornithology's classic disputations. What do the birds use— beak or feet—to break off the twigs they use to build their nests? According to Winsor Marrett Tyler, contributing to *Life Histories*, Louis Agassiz Fuertes, the great observer and illustrator, depicted the bird using its feet, but ornithologist Elliott Coues argued in 1897 that "the bird secured the object with its beak, as it dashed past on wing at full speed." However, "Mr. Fuertes vouched for the correctness of his representation," writes Tyler, so Coues opened up the question by means of "a query inserted in one of our popular periodicals, asking for information." The periodical was—what else?—*The Nidologist*, and Coues's query elicited six replies, five of which were in accord with his opinion.

Case closed. Case reopened, writes Tyler, thirty years later, when ornithologist L. O. Shelley, after thirteen years of devoted study, asserted unequivocally that swifts gather nesting material with their feet, and that he had never in all his years of observation seen otherwise. Considering that Audubon also had described swifts using their feet to snap the twig from the branch, Tyler was prepared to put the question to rest—with some hedging: "Although without much doubt swifts pluck off twigs with their feet, they may find it convenient to arrive at the nest site with their feet free to grasp the wall of the chimney. To gain this end, it is possible that on the way to the nest, the birds may transfer the twig to their beak."

How soon these great controversies are obscured under the dusty cloak of history! From the phlegmatic observations of contemporary commentators (all of whom agree, by the way, that the swifts use their feet), you'd never guess the volume of ink spilled in this debate. The no-nonsense *Birds of North America Online* is typical: "Both parents independently build nest; break off small twigs with feet while flying through branches; return to nest with twig in bill." Ho-hum.

Given the difficulty of seeing into a dark chimney, you might anticipate some lively debate as to what the birds do with the twigs when they get there. But somehow everybody seems to have known from time immemorial exactly what they do: Using saliva from their "seasonally enlarged sublingual glands" (in the language of *Birds of North America Online*), they stick the twigs to the interior wall of the chimney, and to each other, in the shape of a cozy half-hammock, in which the female lays her four or five pure white eggs. (Just about any interior wall will do, actually—open wells, cisterns, uninhabited barns or houses, or, in one case cited by Tyler, "the inside of a door to an outhouse, which, despite its being in regular use, proved successful.")

It's a precarious existence for the hatchlings—naked, blind, and, as Tyler puts it, "no bigger than your fingernail, lying in a frail cradle of sticks that overhangs a black 'drop into nothing.'" The security of that cradle depends more than anything else upon dry weather. The birds have to postpone building during a rainy spell, and even after the nest is built, says Forbush, "sometimes copious rains later dissolve the gluey substance and precipitate nest and eggs or young to the bottom of the chimney."

If they haven't been washed away in the meantime, the young open their eyes at about two weeks and shortly thereafter begin crawling out of the nest, working on their clinging technique. Gradually they make their way upward toward the world of light and air. In the days just before takeoff, writes Audubon, "they scramble up the walls to near the mouth of the chimney, where they are fed." We know this is going on, he says, because we can see "the parents passing close over them, without entering the funnel." It's also at this point, at least in my experience, that the clamoring of the young for food, perhaps enhanced by the chimney's acoustics, is as loud as a thousand nighttime crickets. At four weeks old, the young are ready to assume their airborne existence.

Once the young have fledged, the swifts' gregarious nature takes over. The family from my chimney, for example, might get together with the family from my neighbor's, and several such families will take up temporary roosting quarters in a larger "staging chimney" in the area. By summer's end, the swifts have massed together in tremendous flocks for their migratory journey back to South America, and apparently their roosting behavior at this juncture is something to behold. Picture thousands of swifts beginning to circle at dusk over some suitably large chimney, like maybe in an abandoned factory— "a twittering, funnel-shaped cloud." As darkness comes on, writes

Austin, "they drop, still twittering, from the base of the funnel shape they have formed, into the chimney."

Yes, literally thousands. A single roosting flock of 10,000 has been observed in Kansas, and, in the days before huge industrial chimneys, Audubon discovered a flock of approximately 9,000 roosting in a dead, hollowed-out sycamore tree. It's odd to think, isn't it, in these days of heightened environmental consciousness, that the swifts no longer need to find trees like that great sycamore. As Tyler puts it, "Of the very few birds that benefited by the spread of civilization across the continent, none benefited as much as the chimney swift." Man-made structures, he writes, increased the bird's potential nesting and roosting sites "a millionfold." Consequently, people in even the most densely developed urban areas can witness what Tyler calls, from our point of view, "the most spectacular event in the swift's life," when, during the autumn migration, "the birds, late in the afternoon, congregate in a large, wheel-shaped flock and circle about the chimney they have selected as their roosting place for the night."

Sipping wine on my front porch, enclosed almost to the point of claustrophobia by the fragrant, heavy-leaved forest of summer, I'll have to imagine it. But I don't have to imagine the pair of swifts that have decided that my chimney looks like a place they can call home for the season. I'll watch them every evening, terrorizing the mosquitoes and forcing the paper wasps to crouch low and fearful on their nests. I'll listen for one of the wonderful sounds of summer, which sometimes, in Tyler's lovely image, "when the birds are very high in the air . . . comes down to our ears, softened by distance — like sparks slowly falling to the earth after a rocket has burst."

Northern Mockingbird
Mimus polyglottos

What we have given up to live in the woods — proximity to mall and movie theater, for example — is for the most part negligible. But one of the things we do sorely miss is the song of the mockingbird. This is another bird, like the robin and the blue jay, that has come to prefer the amenities of civilization — its cleared fields and lawns, its gardens and orchards, and its open spaces. Of course, I still see the mockingbird and hear it in town or on the golf course, but how I would love to listen to its song here in the woods on moonlit nights.

Since the time of Mark Catesby, who gave the "mock-bird" its name in 1731, there has never been any question that the mockingbird's voice is its greatest asset. The bird is not modest about its gift; everybody has heard it sing its varied phrases from some conspicuous perch, whether treetop or telephone wire, but you would have to follow an individual mockingbird around for a long time — for its entire life, actually — to hear its complete repertoire.

Charlotte Green writes that not all mockingbirds are equally blessed. Some have no powers of imitation, while others can perfectly repeat a song heard only once. One of her ornithologist friends, she says, knew of a mockingbird that had mastered eighty songs, "including that of a bartramian sandpiper, whose song it could only have heard as it migrated far overhead." A contributor to *Life Histories* reported hearing the mocker giving the summer tanager's *picky-tucky-tuck* call note, then the tanager song, then the call note again, obviously making some association between the two. Even more impressive, this was before the tanager's spring arrival (in Charleston), so the mockingbird was evidently remembering the tune from six months earlier. In fact, ornithologists today maintain that a male mockingbird's repertoire often contains more than 150 distinct song types and that the number generally increases with age. The birds continue to learn new songs not only from other birds, but also by imitating a variety of nonbird animals and even mechanical sounds.

While scientists marvel at the technical ability of this "many-tongued mimic," more poetically inclined souls pay tribute to the sheer beauty of the bird's songs. Here's how Forbush, crowning the mockingbird "the king of song," describes the male's musical ecstasy during courtship: "On moonlit nights at this season the inspired singer launches himself far into the air, filling the silver spaces of the night with the exquisite swells and trills, liquid and sweet, of his unparalleled melody . . . and so he serenades his mate throughout the livelong night."

Then there's the story of Edward Bok, who, insisting on only the finest musical talent for his fabulous Bok Tower Gardens in Lake Wales, Florida, imported caged nightingales from Europe. Much to his surprise, writes Oliver Austin, "the local Mockingbirds were soon singing the same lovely liquid notes." Sound spectrograph records showed the mockingbirds' versions to be exact reproductions of the nightingales'—"each phrase in all its parts, including vibrations beyond the range of the human ear." Alexander Sprunt repeats the story in *Life Histories*, with this nice addendum: "It is said that the European performers were put to silence and soon refused to sing at all."

Audubon, also comparing the American virtuoso to the European, pays characteristically effusive homage to our native songster: "Some [European naturalists] have described the notes of the Nightingale as occasionally fully equal to those of our bird. I have frequently heard both species in confinement, and in the wild state, and without prejudice, have no hesitation in pronouncing the notes of the European Philomel equal to those of a *soubrette* of taste, which, could she study under a Mozart, might perhaps in time become very interesting in her way. But to compare her essays to the finished talent of the Mocking Bird, is, in my opinion, quite absurd."*

What accounts for the "infinite variety" of the mockingbird's song? It can only be love. Research has shown that the female is attracted to the male with the most impressive musical repertoire, a situation to which we poor human males can offer many an analogy. Bird writers, too, tend to agree that the mockingbird in love is at his

---

*The *soubrette* plays the role of maidservant or lady's maid in an opera or musical.

musical best. Audubon again: "See how he flies round his mate, with motions as light as those of the butterfly! . . . His beautiful wings are gently raised, he bows to his love, and again bouncing upwards, opens his bill, and pours forth his melody, full of exultation at the conquest which he has made." More prosaically, *The Birds of North America Online* confirms that song is integral to the male's "flight display": Singing all the while, the male jumps upward, flaps his wings enough to ascend a few feet above the perch, and then parachutes down, wings open, onto the same or a nearby perch. He flashes his white wing patches to add to the allure of the unceasing song. Who could resist?

But as our own species can attest, if love inspires song, so does the lack thereof. The odd fact is that unmated mockingbirds sing more than mated males do. Is this because they are working all the harder to acquire that mate, or because they have given themselves over to singing the blues? Who knows? But in a number of experiments, only unmated males were heard to sing between the hours of midnight and 4:00 A.M. My guess is that nobody's going to find a mate at that hour—at least not one you'd take home to Mama—but that a sweet song might ease the burden of loneliness. Add in the fact that these single, late-night singers tend to tune up during a full moon, and you've got a scene right out of "Heartbreak Hotel."

Actually, I'm still oversimplifying. Or overanthropomorphizing. It's not just love, or its absence, that conjures the mockingbird's song. When a male brings a twig to the nest site, he sings. When he's foraging for insects, he sings. The bird even sings when he's got food in his mouth. The mockingbird is a singing fool, plain and simple.

Yet sentimentalists may be forgiven for believing the mockingbird's best music to be inspired by love. These birds form strong attachments and remain monogamous not merely through the mating season but often for life. Second only to their music, mockingbirds are most famous for their fierce defense of home and hearth. They

Northern Mockingbird (John James Audubon, The Birds of America, vols. 1–4, Special Collections, University Library System, University of Pittsburgh)

take on all comers, writes Sprunt, and "rival the kingbird" in attacking anything that violates their space. Snakes, rodents, hawks, and even human intruders have felt the wrath of the mockingbird who believes its eggs or young threatened.

About the female's solicitude, Audubon says if she returns to the nest to find that even one egg has been somehow moved or displaced, "she utters a low mournful note, at the sound of which the male immediately joins her, and they are both seen to condole together." But he refutes the belief that the female will abandon the nest under such conditions. "On the contrary, she redoubles her assiduity and care. . . . Nay, if the eggs are on the eve of being hatched, she will almost suffer a person to lay hold of her."

It seems a true partnership. The male helps select the nest site, brings in material, and sometimes begins the project before leaving most of the construction to his mate. While incubation remains the female's job, both parents feed the young, one waiting with a grub or caterpillar in its bill until the other leaves, then taking its turn at the nest. Also, both continue to feed the young after they've left the nest, and when the second brood comes along (as it will in this species), the two parents continue to divide up the responsibilities. After helping feed the first fledglings for a few days, the male turns his attention to constructing the foundation for the next nest. When that work is done, he resumes taking care of the young, and the female finishes the nest, then lays and incubates the next set of eggs. And so on, through a long love season that often produces three nests full of young.

Consort as they might, however, the mated pair does not do the hokey-pokey. I refer to the strange dance of the mockingbirds, in which two birds, standing exactly opposite each other about a foot apart, hop up and down, then glide to one side and back again. They might repeat this step, or, in a variation, still facing each other, they might hop sideways, one following the lead of the other, then hop back to their original position. The dance was long assumed to be a courtship ritual, until more attentive observation revealed that the partners in the dance were in most cases two males. Ornithologists today understand the phenomenon to be a territorial face-off. These "boundary dances," according to Derrickson and Breitwisch's report in *The Birds of North America Online*, "can continue in one direction along the territorial boundary, even forcing the two males to dance through or over a shrub or tree and then on to the ground on the other side. In suburban habitat, dances also occur up and over low buildings." The dance takes place in silence, making this one of the few times in the male mockingbird's life when he is not singing.

"SHOOT ALL THE BLUE JAYS YOU WANT, if you can hit 'em," Atticus tells Scout and Jem in Harper Lee's classic novel of the Deep South, "but remember it's a sin to kill a mockingbird."

In fact, this bird is so much a part of southern lore and landscape that "northern mockingbird" seems an odd misnomer. Few southern writers have failed to pay their respects to the mockingbird, and five southern states — Florida, Tennessee, Mississippi, Texas, and Arkansas — have designated it their state bird. Austin scarcely overstates the case when he declares the bird "as symbolic of the Old South as magnolias, hominy, 'chitlins,' and mint juleps."

Yet "the nightingale of the South" sings its sweet song all over North America, and it's doubtful that any writer has been more inspired by this bird than Walt Whitman, way up there on the shore of Long Island. His "Out of the Cradle Endlessly Rocking" tells the story of "two feathered guests from Alabama," the he-bird and the she-bird, and the rapt attention of the "curious boy, never too close, never disturbing them, / Cautiously peering, absorbing, translating." When, inexplicably, the female fails to return to the nest, the male pours out his song to the sea, pleading for the return of his love. The boy, listening, hears his own fateful summons:

Is it indeed toward your mate you sing? or is it really to me?
For I, that was a child, my tongue's use sleeping, now I have
    heard you,
Now in a moment I know what I am for, I awake,
And already a thousand singers, a thousand songs, clearer, louder
    and more sorrowful than yours,

A thousand warbling echoes have started to life within me, never
   to die. . . .
The messenger there arous'd the fire, the sweet hell within,
The unknown want, the destiny of me.

Can't you just hear Audubon? "Mr. Keats's 'Ode to a Nightingale'
might be considered of some interest in its own way, but to compare
it to the finished artistry of the Whitman poem is, in my opinion,
utterly ridiculous."

· · · · · · · · ·

GOATSUCKERS
Caprimulgidae

Whip-Poor-Will
Caprimulgus vociferous

Chuck-Will's-Widow
Caprimulgus carolinensis

Okay, they don't really suck goats, but it's a good enough story to have been around for centuries. Choate says it goes back at least to Aristotle, who wrote, "Flying to the udders of she-goats, it sucks them, and thus gets its name [*Caprimulgus*]. They say that the udder withers when it has sucked at it, and that the goat goes blind." Austin suggests that the root of the "ancient fallacy" lay in these birds' huge mouths, but that doesn't do it for me. What? Just because they *could* do it, they did it, or were presumed to, no matter how improbable? That's like calling human beings "earth destroyers" just because . . . ooops. Never mind.

The members of the family familiar to us in the East are the whip-poor-will (*Caprimulgus vociferous*, or "noisy goatsucker"); the chuck-will's-widow (*Caprimulgus carolinensis*, or "goatsucker of Carolina," where Catesby first found the bird); and the nighthawk (*Chordeiles minor*, which means something else altogether*). They also go by the family name "nightjars," which, if less colorful, is more literally apt. These birds are best known for their nighttime vocals, loud and repetitive enough to jar us out of the deepest slumber.

The whip-poor-will and the chuck-will's-widow are supposed to whistle their names, which is a useful enough way to distinguish them if you remember that the whip-poor-will deemphasizes its second syllable (WHIP-poor-WILL) and that the chuck-will's-widow emphasizes its. It also stretches that second syllable out, so that, in my

---

*Paraphrasing Choate, *Chordeiles* might be rendered "circling about in the evening," a reference to the bird's insect-hunting habits; *minor* refers to its smaller size, compared with the European nightjar.

103

opinion, the name would more accurately match the call if it were "chuck-widow's-will" (chuck-WIDOW'S-WILL), but I suppose syntacticians would take offense.

Both birds have become infamous for their ability to repeat their calls endlessly and without pause. "Regularly at half past seven in one part of the summer," wrote Thoreau, "the whippoorwills chanted their vespers for half an hour, sitting on a stump by my door, or upon the ridge pole of the house. . . . They sang at intervals throughout the night, and were again as musical as ever just before and about dawn." Austin says that for several springs running, a whip-poor-will made his doorstep its favorite calling perch and that he would put himself to sleep counting the repetitions. "My record count was 402 Whip-poor-wills, repeated a second apart, before the bird stopped or I went to sleep." A southern friend, he says, counted 834 successive chuck-will's-widow calls, then adds that "the all-time high seems to be John Burroughs' record of hearing a bird 'lay upon the back of poor Will' 1,088 blows in succession."

Austin fails to note whether or not John Burroughs had to be institutionalized after listening to this record-setting performance. One thousand eighty-eight? Granted, the male has to use his call to establish the boundaries of his territory and attract his mate, but after a while, who's going to be attracted? Is any sane woman going to go out with a guy who calls her on the telephone, nonstop, from sundown until nine-thirty and then again from three o'clock till dawn? I don't think so. (Sorry. More misplaced anthropomorphizing. Now I find in *The Birds of North America Online* that the males who sing longest and loudest are the ones who've lost their mates.)

The nighthawk, by the way, has a nasal flight cry — *peeent, peeent* — that sounds nothing like the other two. In fact, Peterson calls this bird the aberrant member of the family, and on that note I am willing to let it go, with one final comment: Of the three, the nighthawk is the only one I've ever seen. You probably have, too, if you've ever been to

Whip-Poor-Will (John James Audubon, The Birds of America, vols. 1–4, Special Collections, University Library System, University of Pittsburgh)

a twilight baseball game in the summer. As the sky darkens and the stadium floodlights begin to illuminate the field, you're likely to see two or three of them, swooping and turning on their pointed, swept-back wings, gorging themselves on all those plump, helpless moths.

As for the whip-poor-will and the chuck-will's-widow, their audibility is fully matched by their invisibility. As Tyler puts it in *Life Histories*, everyone recognizes the song of the whip-poor-will, but how many have ever seen it or would recognize it if they did see it? "Not, it may be presumed, one-tenth of 1 percent." Since these nocturnal creatures feed on flying insects and since such insects are attracted to light, I guess I might catch a glimpse of one if I erected a security light like many of my neighbors have along our semirural road. But our security is provided by a closed gate, a long driveway, and two loud dogs, and we like our nights to be as dark as nature allows; so we're not likely to see these birds chasing moths through any circle of lamplight. (On the other hand, we have no security against mosquitoes, another favorite food, so maybe a tiki lamp or two would be worth considering.)

In any case, we are for sure not going to see these birds during the day. When it comes to camouflage, the bobwhite has nothing on the whip-poor-will or the chuck-will's-widow. Plus, while the bobwhite must bestir itself to conduct its business during normal business hours, "whip" and "chuck" lie motionless all the livelong day. They might conceal themselves on the leafy ground or else, as Forbush puts it, "horizontally on a limb, looking like some sort of knot or growth of the tree." Thus woven into the woodland tapestry, they snooze away the day, like owls, bats, vampires, and other creatures of the dark.

These masters of concealment build no nest but lay their two eggs directly on the forest's natural bed of dead leaves and pine needles. The eggs, creamy white with blotches of brown, are "conspicuous when exposed," says Harrison; but the parents don't allow much exposure, and the incubating bird is pretty much invisible. The same

Chuck-Will's-Widow (John James Audubon, The Birds of America, vols. 1–4, Special Collections, University Library System, University of Pittsburgh)

applies to the hatchlings, which come genetically equipped for their life of obscurity. The little chick, writes Tyler, "finds itself lying on the ground, with dead leaves all about. The dead leaves look like the chick, and the chick looks like the dead leaves; no one can tell them apart; practically the chick *is* a dead leaf, and, although hatched, it is still invisible, just as it was when hidden in the egg."

Of course, it's possible to stumble accidentally upon one of these birds' nests, a circumstance that has given rise to a dispute about their behavior. Audubon claimed to have seen a chuck-will's-widow, after its nest was intruded upon, pick her eggs up in her mouth and move them to another location. Later writers (Austin, Forbush) accepted the story and attributed this rare ability to the goatsucker family in general. But others—like Tyler, Harrison, and most contemporary experts—demand more evidence. Apparently, in dire straights, these birds have been known to move their eggs by rolling them a short distance, but picking them up in their mouths? Doubtful.

Since this theory, like the one that gave the family its name, seems to have its origin in the birds' remarkably large mouths, it's time to ask: Just how big are those things? Actually, in both species the bill is quite small and weak, but both birds do have the ability to open wide. As *The Birds of North America Online* reports, the "enormous gape (36–37 millimeters)" of the whip-poor-will "allows insects up to 50 millimeters long to be swallowed." And the whip-poor-will is the smaller of the two species. The chuck-will's-widow, some 2 to 3 inches longer (12 inches vs. 9½) and with a gape correspondingly more gaping, cannot only gobble down the largest of moths but, according to *Life Histories*, sometimes swallows whole such small birds as warblers, hummingbirds, and sparrows. (It is assumed that the bird must afterward "cast a pellet," like the owl does, but the chuck-will's-widow is so secretive that nobody knows for sure.)

Still, both species feed almost exclusively on nocturnal insects, especially moths. Apparently needing some faint light to pursue their prey, they take to wing at dusk and again at dawn—unless the moon is full, in which case they feed all night long. With the long bristles around their mouths acting as a kind of funnel, they cut here and there through the air, low over the ground across open fields, or skim the tops of shrubs or trees, inhaling the insects by the hundreds. Audubon adds the curious note that "even the largest moths on which [these birds] feed are always swallowed tail foremost."

Temporarily satiated, a bird might pause to sing for a while, for which purpose it apparently prefers a light-colored, flat, open space, maybe even a farmhouse doorstep. So is it possible after all, on moonlit nights in particular, to catch a glimpse of one of these birds? It is, says Tyler, especially given their habit of following the same route every evening — "a stone wall, a low branch, or a certain spot on the ground — where they are almost sure to stop and sing for a while." But you've got to watch closely, "for, although in flight it looms big even in the dusk, when it comes to rest, with a flip of its wings it becomes a bit of dead wood, a clod of earth, or vanishes altogether."

Leaving only that voice echoing through the night. An omen of death in the lore of many cultures, for unmarried women in ancient Europe the cry of the whip-poor-will might presage an even worse fate. According to the legend, one call meant the woman wouldn't marry for at least a year. Two, the hoped-for number, meant impending matrimony. If the bird called three times or more, the woman was doomed to spinsterhood.

The good news? If the bird called 1,008 times, all bets were off.

Ruby-Throated Hummingbird
Archilochus colubris

Here in mid-August, the hummingbirds are so constantly at the feeder that it seems like I'm filling it up every other day. It hangs on a hook attached to the deck rail in back of the house, just a few feet from where Dede and I like to sip our morning coffee and read the paper. They come humming in right over our heads, sounding like mutant bumblebees, except they're so close we can also hear their squeaky twitter.

This morning we had three at once—humming, squeaking, sipping, flying off, flying back—and I had to wonder if they were already trying to fatten themselves up for their southward migration. It would seem too early; I know we still see them here well into fall. But Burleigh writes that the males "depart for their winter quarters much earlier than the females or young of the year" and that during his long years of observation in Georgia, he "never noted an adult male later than the latter part of July."

Maybe the male I'm watching right now, sitting impatiently on the hook from which I've removed the feeder to refill it once again, is in fact trying to fatten up so he can hit the highway and catch up with his pals. Or maybe, since we're having one of the hottest, driest summers on record, he and all the other hummers are just thirsty. In any case, they'll all be gone soon enough, headed to Central America on a journey that will include a 500-mile, nonstop flight across the Gulf of Mexico. The energy they build up for the trip often doubles their body weight, yet even so, the feat seems pretty miraculous. Austin says that a physiologist once proved by metabolic tests in his laboratory that the ruby-throat couldn't possibly store enough fuel within its tiny frame for such a lengthy flight, but, he writes, "the birds, never having read the report, continue to do so twice each year."[*]

---

[*]According to Scott Weidensaul in *The Birder's Miscellany*, "Some hummingbirds may hitchhike south. A number of reports, most of them anecdotal, tell of migrating geese being shot which, on closer examination, were found to have torpid hummingbirds nestled beneath their back feathers."

In fact, there's little that isn't amazing about this exquisite creature. We've all noticed that it beats its wings so rapidly (more than fifty times per second) that we can't really see them move, but it's the unique way the wing bone attaches to the shoulder that enables the hummer to fly in any direction it wants, including straight backward. Or, as we've all seen, it can hover, which affords it a further unusual ability. Using its long needlelike bill, it can pause in midair to sip the nectar of tubular flower blossoms whose petals would not be able to support it if it tried to alight.

It's a common misconception, though, that flower nectar is the hummingbird's only food. Audubon observed that it wasn't so much the nectar the birds were after but, rather, the tiny insects inside the flower blossoms—"the nectar or honey which they sip from the different flowers, being of itself insufficient to support them." To prove the point, he cited experiments in which birds in confinement, fed exclusively on sugar water, died of emaciation within a few months, whereas others who were brought fresh flowers from wood or garden (with the insect component intact) lived twelve months and then were released. Later writers have confirmed Audubon's observation—and expanded it. The hummers not only eat the insects they find in flower blossoms; they eat a wide variety of bugs—mosquitoes, spiders, gnats, fruit flies, small bees—wherever they can find them, including midair, where they take them flycatcher-style.

Audubon may have veered toward hyperbole, though, in his tender description of the male's courtship behavior. "How quickly he dives towards a flower, and returns with a loaded bill, which he offers to her to whom alone he feels desirous of being united; . . . how, soon after, the blissful compact is sealed; how, then, the courage and care of the male are redoubled; how he even dares to give chase to the Tyrant Fly-catcher, hurries the Blue-bird and the Martin to their boxes, and how, on sounding pinions, he joyously returns to the side of his lovely mate." All these are "proofs of the sincerity, fidelity, and courage" of the male, as well as of "the care he will take of her."

Hmmmm. As Jake tells Brett in the final line of *The Sun Also Rises*, "Isn't it pretty to think so." In fact, the male's utter disregard for his

mate, postcopulatory, is another of this bird's unique characteristics. *Life Histories* states the case plainly: "Mating, in the ordinary sense of the word . . . appears not to take place. . . . I have found no evidence that a male's interest in a female one day is manifested towards the same female the following day. All the pretty ways common among many species of mated pairs, often lasting two months at least, are entirely lacking among Hummingbirds. The male appears to be a free lance whose intimate interest in the female is confined to the short period just before and during egg-laying."

Not that the male is anything less than a spectacular suitor. I have been fortunate enough to witness his fabulous courtship display, in which he swings wildly back and forth in a U-shaped arc, with his ruby throat feathers, or gorget, ablaze in the sunlight. The performance took place just off our front porch, as though it were intended for me, but no doubt there was a female perched in the nandina, close to level with the bottom of his arc, mesmerized. Unable to resist this blandishment, she'll fly to him for their in-air consummation, "after which," as Austin puts it, "the male loses interest in his partner."

Some suspect the male of polygamy, but whether or not he seeks out another love interest, one thing is clear: He's a classic deadbeat dad. In Forbush's words, the male "becomes a gay wanderer with nothing to do but to enjoy himself or to chase other birds. He spends much time sitting on a particular twig, which he chooses for his watch-tower and resting-place, and dressing his plumage, while his mate builds the nest and rears the brood."

The good news is that the female needs no help, and the nest she builds on her own is a masterpiece of craftsmanship. Scarcely more than an inch across and an inch deep, it's covered with lichen on the outside and lined with the softest materials nature can supply, like milkweed or thistle down. The whole thing is stitched together with spider silk, which, when you think about it, just can't be all that easy to work with. My sister Nettie e-mailed me a series of digital

Ruby-Throated Hummingbird (John James Audubon, The Birds of America, vols. 1–4, Special Collections, University Library System, University of Pittsburgh)

photographs that chronicled the whole parenting process — from the mother sitting on her two white eggs to the fledging of the young a month later. These were amazing pictures and, since this was an Allen's hummingbird, a resident of the California coast, a tribute to the info-potential of the Internet. But most impressive of all was the interior of the nest, which looked padded with pure cotton.

As *Life Histories* points out, a bird of such small size is bound to court unusual dangers. Sometimes, for instance, their use of spider-web backfires, and they become hopelessly entangled. It's also been reported that hummers flying low over water have been snatched out of the air by hungry bass or even, closer to shore, by bullfrogs. Stranger still, one observer saw a hummer taken down by a huge dragonfly that landed on the bird's back and "seized it by the neck." The witness managed to drive the dragonfly away, picked up the bird, and held it in the palm of his hand until, after a minute or two, it recovered and flew away. I can add from my own observation that the hummer is careful to keep yellow jackets at a distance and quick to move to the other side of the feeder, or retreat entirely, if one buzzes in too close.

One thing the hummingbird doesn't seem to worry about, though, is other birds — except perhaps other hummingbirds. We've all seen these birds chase one another from the feeder like tiny heat-seeking missiles, and Audubon remarks on their "frequent battles in the air." Still, they seem to have no fear of other bird species, maybe because they're just too damn fast. Forbush says he's seldom heard of a hummer being caught by any other bird (with the possible exception, as we've seen, of the chuck-will's-widow) and adds that the hummers themselves are "quite pugnacious," willing to attack virtually any other bird regardless of size.

I might have doubted this claim if I hadn't just recently watched a hummer repeatedly chasing the titmice and chickadees out of the cherry tree. *Why in the world?* I wondered. With my binoculars I could detect just the faintest ruby splotch on its throat, suggesting that maybe it was an adolescent male who, maybe, was practicing the art of establishing and defending territory. In any case, the titmice and chickadees took the minuscule dive-bomber seriously and sped away without protest. I guess it's not so surprising after all to read in *The Folklore of Birds* that the name of the Aztec god of sun and war, Huitzilopochitli, translates as "hummingbird of the south" or that Aztec warriors hoped to be reincarnated as hummingbirds.

It's also apparent, as Dede and I prove again each morning, that the hummers regard human beings as merely a nuisance to be endured or, worse, a factotum to be employed. We supply our man-made nectar, of course, but that's not all. I was watering my small vegetable garden the other day, letting the fine spray arc to the cucumber plants on the far side a dozen feet away, when a hummer perched on the low wire fence that surrounds the plot to keep the dogs out. She had arrived for a bath, and I was so delighted to see such a thing that I held the hose steady while she fluttered, ruffled, and shook from head to tail. My, but she was enjoying herself, and in no hurry for her pleasure to end. Finally, when it became clear that she would bathe as long as I would serve, I turned the hose to the base of the tomato plants, and she zipped away with not the slightest expression of gratitude.

......

Northern Cardinal
Cardinalis cardinalis[*]

You have to pity the poor cardinal, as common here in the South as the dogwood tree and equally taken for granted. Imagine how you'd holler, though, if you had never seen one before and all of a sudden there he was, in full vermilion splendor, cracking open sunflower seeds on your feeder. Or how about if you were sitting on your front porch at dusk on a summer evening and suddenly heard for the first time, when all the other birds had quieted for the night, this bird's startlingly clear and beautiful whistle.

In fact, the lovely cardinal (whether he or she) freely delivers just about everything you could ask from a bird. "In richness of plumage, elegance of motion, and strength of song," writes Audubon, "this species surpasses all its kindred in the United States." Throw in beneficial feeding habits and well-developed parenting skills, as Bent does, and you've got the complete package.

Not to mention the fact that the cardinal is a year-round resident whose gaudy plumage brightens even the bleakest days of winter. I suppose its conspicuous presence all year long is one of the reasons it seems so ordinary, but I'll never complain about seeing a cardinal catching the winter sun on the bare branches of the cherry tree. There he is in early January, keeping company with the chickadees

[*]Everybody agrees that the cardinal takes its name from the high-ranking church official of the same name, the obvious connection being the red attire of both species. But it occurred to Peter Cashwell, in *The Verb "To Bird,"* to wonder why this native of North America, presumably discovered and named by colonists from Protestant England, would have been, in effect, forced to pay tribute to the Church of Rome. In fact, Cashwell spends some months (including a particularly frustrating trip to the Library of Congress) trying to get to the bottom of this mystery. He finds the answer serendipitously (like birding itself should be, he says) with the discovery of a book called *A Dictionary of Americanisms*. It wasn't the colonists who named the cardinal but, rather, the earlier explorers—La Salle, de Soto, Cartier, Ponce de Leon, Vespucci, and Verrazano—and their sailors and crewmen, who no doubt returned to their Roman Catholic countries with tales of the brilliant bird who wore the vestments of the august officials who select the pope.

Northern Cardinal (John James Audubon, The Birds of America, vols. 1–4, Special Collections, University Library System, University of Pittsburgh)

and titmice, though alone of his kind. It strikes me as curious to see the single male, day after day throughout the month, but this turns out to be typical behavior. Watching a male during this time of year, one of Bent's correspondents noted his hostility to any other cardinal, male or female, that tried to approach the feeder. "An intruding cardinal was either driven off, or it in turn drove off the first. Other and smaller song-birds were, however, tolerated without any threatening movements. In late winter and early spring male birds became much more tolerant of females, and both sexes often fed together."

Sure enough, here she comes in early February, appearing on the ground below the feeder, and from then on she is as regular a visitor as he. By early March we are hearing their lovely evensong: *whit-whit-whit-whit, tuerrr, tuerrr, tuerrr, tuerrr*. I had assumed it was the male, but that's not necessarily so. He may start singing earlier, says Bent, but the female joins him in late February or March. "From then till nesting time the male and female often appear to sing against each other, one singing, then stopping, while the other takes up the song." It's such a clear and pretty whistle that people, too, are tempted to join in. Forbush says one of its notes sounds so much like a man whistling up his dog that faithful canines are frequently fooled into running home to see what's up.

By mid-March they've probably built their nest, which a better birder than I would no doubt be able to find. Though they like to build in thick tangles of shrub or vine, the nest is usually lower than head high, bulky, and, says Burleigh, "seldom well concealed." I watch my pair come and go along the same route every day, out of the woods on the west side of the yard, but I haven't been able to follow them home. (It's my observation, as a matter of fact, that cardinals are unusually shy and flighty birds; they're gone from the feeder if I so much as shift position at my window.)

Actually, it's the female that builds the nest, but the male is attentive, keeping her company during the job and, once she has laid her set of three or four eggs, bringing her food while she incubates. In fact, the female apparently sings from the nest when she's hungry, and the male responds to this auditory cue. According to *The Birds of North America Online*, it may be that this communication allows the visually conspicuous male to stay away when he's not needed and thus minimize the chances of disclosing the nest's location to predators.

If the female is sitting on her eggs by late March, her young will have fledged by late April, but the cardinal pair are far from finished with parenting. Throughout their eastern range they will have at least two broods, and here in the South, three is the usual number. Over the course of the long breeding season, the male proves his mettle by helping feed the nestlings and then taking over their care entirely when his mate settles over the eggs of the next brood.

Life Histories correspondent J. Van Tyne gives us an idea of just how demanding this work is. He watched a male with a beak full of green worms gathered up for the young stop at a feeding tray, disgorge the worms onto the shelf, crack and eat some sunflower seeds, pick the worms up again, lay them down again, eat some more seeds, then finally take up the worms and fly off toward the nest. The poor guy was obviously famished.

Probably about the time the first brood was fledging here in my woods, I watched a male foraging on the ground in the uncut grass beyond the feeder, no doubt hunting for worms or insects for his young. Hey, it ain't easy. Ten full minutes of hopping through the weeds produced nothing, and he, like the bird Bent's correspondent describes, had to head up to the feeder to fortify himself before resuming the hunt. The guy is no slacker, as another anecdote from *Life Histories* illustrates: After losing their nest and young in a storm, a pair of cardinals quickly set about rebuilding the nest and filling it with a new clutch of eggs. But before the second brood hatched, the male took on the job of feeding four young robins—working at it every bit as hard as the robin parents.

Of course, breeding season also means territory defense, a job cardinals take seriously. The males establish the territory, often drawing virtually the same boundaries year after year, but both male and female defend it. The male chases other males from the territory exclusively, and the female chases other females—a scenario that, for me at least, suggests an amusing human analogue. As virtually all bird-watchers can testify, cardinals are so aggressive in defense of territory that they often do battle with themselves — reflected in window glass. This is interesting behavior to witness, for a little while. In our case, it goes on all summer at our bedroom window, at the least opportune times. Our male starts as soon as day breaks, jumping around on the window screen a good half-hour before we would normally wake up; then he inevitably resumes the battle in the early afternoon, right after I've stretched out for the mandatory nap.

But, believe me, I'm happy to trade the shut-eye for the company this bird provides. No wonder that in earlier days, as Charlotte Green reports, the cardinal was trapped and sent to Europe as the "Virginia nightingale." Audubon adds that they are relatively easy to raise, and even breed, in captivity, but he cautions that "the purity of its colouring is soon lost when it is kept in confinement." What exporters and importers of the bird may not have known is that for cardinals to maintain high color, they've got to ingest a lot of carotene during their fall molt, a substance they can get from fruits and insects but not from seeds. So if the caged birds of Audubon's acquaintance lost their color, maybe it's because their owners kept them on a diet of "bird seed." Similarly, if during the autumn our (and your) cardinals come less frequently to the feeder, where the pickings are easy, it's because they know, in Yeats's phrase, that "they must labor to be beautiful."

Well, beautiful they are, and inseparable, throughout the long summer. Whether working open sunflower seeds with those fat orange beaks (Audubon calls this bird the Cardinal Grosbeak) or serenading Dede and me from the darkening wood, the male and female are our perfect neighbors: always close by but never too close.

But where are the children? Way back in June, Don Hastings was already asking me if the cardinals were bringing their young to the feeder. He went on and on about it — "just the most wonderful thing to watch" — absolutely lording it over me. I watched in June. I watched in July. In August, it was still the male and female, except now the male was starting to look a little ragged, presumably beginning his fall molt.

Shoot—it occurred to me that I didn't even know what I was looking for. Maybe I was seeing the young without realizing it. I read Peterson: "*Immature*: Similar to the female, but with a blackish bill." Midmorning, mid-August I looked out the window and saw a male at the feeder with what looked like a female fluttering awkwardly at the other side of the dish. I looked through my binoculars. Female-looking, except a little smaller, and a blackish bill.

The bird finally settled on the rim of the feeder, wings still vibrating for balance. Daddy cracked open a sunflower shell and calmly placed the little seed in the open mouth of his youngster.

Summer, you can go now.

Autumn

Wild Turkey
Meleagris gallopavo

The turkeys showed up not long after we moved in, and no wonder. I had just thrown out a bunch of grass seed. Then we got Peanut, our yellow lab (mostly) mix, and since then the only fowl to appear in the yard are the neighborhood chickens she has killed and brought home. Turkey still haunt our woods, though. We occasionally see them meandering across the driveway or hear them gobbling down by the creek.

Two years ago in October, my journal tells me, Peanut and Moses (our other dog of dubious ancestry, who, apparently abandoned on the roadside as a puppy, wandered down our driveway and arrived, after all, in the promised land) dragged what was left of one—blue head, immense wings, tail feathers, feet, and legs—up to the edge of the yard. Only thing gone was all the meat. We'd been hearing coyotes. I saved a couple of tail feathers and then—much to the dogs' distress—threw the carcass on top of a brush pile I was about to set afire. A day later, looking out my upstairs office window, I saw half a dozen turkeys making their deliberate way across the crest of the ridge just past the edge of our clearing. I watched them for an hour; they moved so slowly that they seemed not to be moving at all. Now I know why. When they scratch for food, as these birds were doing, they follow a routine as precise as the fox-trot: Scratch once with the first foot, then with the other twice, again with the first, then one step backward.

Watching through my binoculars I noticed something else: They all had breast beards, meaning that they were probably all male. The breeding season was obviously long over, but still—a bunch of guys?

Wild turkeys have enjoyed a unique distribution cycle. Spanish explorers found these big, flavorful birds in the Americas and hauled them back to Spain, whence they spread across Europe. In sixteenth-century England, they were regarded highly enough to be served as a table delicacy to Henry VIII. A century later, the prudent Pilgrims brought them to the New World, only to find the woods of New En-

Wild Turkey (John James Audubon, The Birds of America, vols. 1–4, Special Collections, University Library System, University of Pittsburgh)

gland resounding with the gobblers' call. (It was while making its way across Europe, by the way, that the bird received its common English name, probably through the erroneous assumption that it had come from Turkey.)

It's well known that Benjamin Franklin believed the useful, attractive, and thoroughly indigenous wild turkey would have made a more appropriate national emblem than the bald eagle. In his day they were plentiful enough to be sold in the marketplace for a penny a pound. But the axes and blunderbusses of the settlers told a predictable tale. Franklin died in 1790; surely he would have been saddened to learn that the bird was gone from New England a half-century later.

Those same causes — overhunting and habitat loss — continued to decimate wild turkey populations in other areas of the country as well, and by the middle of the twentieth century the situation reached its nadir. Here in Georgia, the turkey population was down to just a few thousand birds in the whole state, and reliable estimates put the total number of wild turkeys nationwide at a mere 130,000. In the 1970s, though, captive breeding and relocation programs began to reverse the decline, and by 1980 the count, nationally, was back up to 1.8 million. The population has probably peaked by now, since suitable habitat (which continues to decline, of course) can only support so many birds, but in the meantime the resurgence of the wild turkey is a good thing. This is a bird that bears watching.

Especially during mating season. In mid-February, when the urge takes hold, the female, like a blushing bride-to-be, sequesters herself, apparently as a way to bring the males' desire to a fever pitch. When her built-in basal thermometer says it's time, she calls from the ground, and all the available males promptly descend from their roosts. Now comes the justly famous display: the great puffing out of feathers, the spreading of the fabulous fan-shaped tail, and the drooping and rattling of the wings — to say nothing of the ultimate blandishment, the engorgement of the snood. Throw in the gobbling and the strutting, and you've got a regular Mr. Universe competition.

Given the heat of the moment, writes Audubon, "desperate battles take place, ending in bloodshed, and often in the loss of many lives, the weaker falling under the repeated blows inflicted upon their head by the stronger." In the typical contest the two males move back and forth like a couple of wrestlers, each trying to get the right beak-hold on the other. And woe unto the bird that loses his grip, "for the other," writes Audubon, "still holding fast, hits him violently with spurs and wings, and in a few minutes brings him to the ground. The moment he is dead, the conqueror treads him under foot." Contemporary accounts would make Audubon's seem a mite dramatic. In a more likely scenario, one bird wins the battle by getting his beak around the back of the other's neck and forcing his head to the ground, at which point the loser twists free and slinks away with shrinking snood, and perhaps a final humiliating pop from the victor's wing to send him along.

To the victor go the spoils, which, since the turkey is polygamous, may be more than he bargained for. In *Life Histories* we read that, as the season is under way, the gobbler, up in his roosting tree early in the day, begins to gobble and display, waiting for the approach of spouse no. 1. When she sounds her responsive "yelp," he flies down to the ground, struts and gobbles again, and does his cockly duty. "He probably knows how many hens he has in his harem," writes Bent, "and keeps on strutting and gobbling until he has served them all. He roosts in the vicinity and repeats the performance every day until the laying season is over or until he becomes emaciated and takes no further interest in the hens." Until, in other words, the poor boy is *spent*.

Audubon's picture of the males in this condition evokes a kind of a post-honeymoon familiarity: Now the toms "become clumsy and slovenly, if one may say so, cease to fight with each other, give up gobbling or calling so frequently, and assume so careless a habit, that the hens are obliged to make all the advances themselves. They *yelp* loudly and almost continually for the cocks, run up to them, caress them, and employ various means to rekindle their expiring ardour."

Too late. The fire is out. The snood sags over the beak most pathetically. But now the hen has more important things to do—like make a nest and raise her young. It's difficult work and fraught with peril.

Since her nest is on the ground, her eggs and—four weeks later—her hatchlings will be vulnerable. So she builds her nest in secret, covers it with leaves when she has to be away, and always approaches it from a different direction. The crow is not the only enemy that might be watching. Oddly, in a remarkably un-Darwinian twist, the old tom will destroy his own get if he comes across the nest. Audubon says he does this "for the purpose of protracting his sexual enjoyments," but hasn't he already had all the enjoyments he can stand? Perhaps he anticipates rivals in the coming generation.

In the meantime, the female is a wary and protective mother. She'll feign injury to lure predators—including the human variety—away from her nest. Or sometimes several hens will lay together, using a common nest, so that at least one will always be available for guard duty. In the days right after hatching, with the precocial chicks already leaving the nest, the mother's greatest fear appears to be rainy weather. Audubon says that turkeys are scarce after a particularly rainy spring because "if once completely wetted, the young seldom recover." If the chicks do get wet, he adds, "the mother, like a skilful physician, plucks the buds of the spice-wood bush, and gives them to her young."

I've had trouble verifying this marvelous bit of turkey behavior. Bent doesn't mention it in *Life Histories*. Forbush says only that Audubon makes note of it. I do know that spicebush, as we call it, produces tasty red berries enjoyed by a variety of birds and animal life. Here's what I didn't know but have found out, thanks to "Wildman" Steve Brill's *Identifying and Harvesting Edible and Medicinal Plants in Wild (and Not So Wild) Places*: Pioneers called spicebush "fever bush" and used a decoction of its bark to induce sweating, activate the immune system, and expel toxins. Indians, likewise, drank an infusion to ward off colds, coughs, croup, and measles. That's enough to convince me of the plant's effectiveness against wetness in infant turkeys, so let's take Audubon at his word and give Mama some credit.

Maybe it's their early aversion to the damp that makes turkeys so fond of sun- and dust-bathing. They love to lie on one side and stretch the opposite wing out to catch the rays, and if they're still looking for fun, they'll find a deserted anthill to roll around in. Audubon says this last activity has the added benefit of preventing infestation by ticks and other vermin, "these insects being unable to bear the odour of the earth in which ants have been."*

If they survive to adulthood, turkeys get big enough to be safe from most predators other than humans. Peanut wouldn't take one on, I don't think. At least she doesn't try to climb the trees where they roost, like she does when she's after a raccoon. A wildcat will lie in wait for one, they say, but how many wildcats do you see these days? Roosting on their high limbs at night, about the only thing turkeys have to worry about is the great horned owl, which won't hesitate to take down one several times its own size. But if we'll take Audubon's word for it one more time, the turkeys have got this menace figured out, too. Alerted by a warning "cluck" from one of their number, the turkeys keep their eyes on "the murderer" as he reconnoiters. The owl selects its victim and "comes down upon it like an arrow," but at the last second the targeted turkey will "lower its head, stoop, and spread its tail in an inverted manner over its back, by which action the aggressor is met by a smooth inclined plane, along which it glances without hurting the Turkey; immediately after which the latter drops to the ground, and thus escapes, merely with the loss of a few feathers."

I don't doubt it. If you live outside, as Audubon did for years at a time, there's no telling what you might see — even at night.

Meanwhile, back to those six males making their slow way across my hardwood ridge in early October. Now we know: With the mating season over, they had been shunned by the protective mother birds, who would have no further use for the tired toms for the next four months or so. And that occasional single gobble from the creek bottom on a late summer evening? Just old loneliness coming down, maybe, or the recollection of good times gone by.

---

*Actually, the turkey's habit of rolling around in an anthill must certainly be a form of the bird behavior now known as "anting," which is covered in some detail in the essay on the blue jay.

·········

Canada Goose
Branta canadensis

It seems amazing now, but it wasn't until sometime in the mid-1980s, when I was somewhere in my mid-thirties, that I saw a Canada goose for the first time. A small flock of them, actually, waddled through a brown hayfield beside a cow pond on a farm in northwest Georgia. It was a thrill to finally see the big, handsome bird with the conspicuous white chin strap set against its jet-black head and neck. (There are other possibilities, but *Branta* may derive from Old English *brant*, or burnt, a reference to the charred-black coloration of the goose's upper parts.)

Ten years later, you couldn't walk out the door without tripping over a Canada goose, or so it seemed in my neck of the woods. During most of the 1990s, I worked at a little book publishing company located in an office park amid the sprawl just north of Atlanta. It was an undistinguished property in every respect — some fifteen or so one-story buildings, each long enough to house several office suites, scattered throughout the little maze of "parkway." It did have one small swath of greensward, though, and, at the far side of it, an uninviting little pond the source of whose water was anybody's guess. But that little stretch of fescue and that little puddle of water was all it took. The place was covered up in Canada geese. Every fall, when the managers of the complex hosted the annual barbecue for the tenants, the women in our office were reluctant to go for fear of stepping in goose shit.

"I have never heard of an instance of their breeding in the Southern States," wrote Audubon, "the extreme heat being entirely uncongenial to their constitution." When he was writing, and for a century or so thereafter, the southern limit of the Canada goose's breeding range was set at the 35th parallel, a line that would have excluded the Deep South states of Louisiana, Mississippi, Alabama, Georgia, and Florida. But introductions and translocations over the past few decades have shown the goose's constitution to be more adaptable than Audubon imagined, and these birds now breed in every part of the

Canada Goose (John James Audubon, The Birds of America, *vols. 1–4, Special Collections, University Library System, University of Pittsburgh)*

North American continent. What's more, many of the now-southern birds (like so many transplants of the human kind) have decided they like it enough to stay year-round and, in the language of ornithologists, "have lost the migratory habit."

For the most part, though, Canada geese remain impressive migrators; they fly a long way, and they like to get there early. As Forbush, writing in Massachusetts, puts it, "Wild geese are the forerunners of winter and the harbingers of spring. While ice still covers our lakes, before even the wood frogs begin to croak, when the spring floods first begin to break up the frozen rivers, the geese are on their way. . . . Not even the first call of the Bluebird so stirs the blood of the listener." Thoreau, also in Massachusetts, heard them going the other way, "lumbering in . . . with a clangor and whistling of wings . . . some to alight in Walden and some flying low over the woods toward Fair Haven, bound for Mexico," and was glad to have just finished plastering the walls of his cabin.

Not only are the Canada geese early arrivals on their breeding grounds; they mated before they left. Audubon speculates that the northern summer is so short, there's no time for fooling around once they get there. He also describes, with characteristic relish, the fascinating particulars of the Canada goose's mating game. After a gander has defeated a rival in a battle that might last a half-hour, he advances toward the female, his head no more than an inch from the ground, bill open, hissing loudly, as he shakes his quills and feathers. With his neck curving and twisting amorously, he circles around her, and she demonstrates her acceptance by curving her neck likewise. But all of a sudden the defeated male decides to give it another go. The lover tries to ignore the new challenge, but when struck by the rival's wing, "the affront cannot be borne in the presence of so large a company." In the end, "the mated gander has caught hold of his antagonist's head with his bill; no bull-dog could cling faster to his victim; he squeezes him with all the energy of rage, lashes him with his powerful wings, and at length drives him away, spreads out his pinions, runs with joy to his mate, and fills the air with cries of exultation." (In fact, *Birds of North America Online* describes the celebration between the victorious male and his mate as the "Triumph Ceremony"—a "central behavior" in these birds' social organization, as it establishes and secures family and pair bonds.)

The gander's ferocity is appropriate. After all, this is the mate he has chosen for life. In *The Courtship of Birds*, Hilda Simon writes that the Canada goose "is as fine an example of a faithful mate and devoted parent as one can find among birds. . . . The pair bond among Canada geese is so strong that they do indeed stay together 'until death does them part.'" What's more, if one of the pair does die, the bereaved is in no hurry to find a replacement. Simon cites one case of a gander who, having lost his mate, "remained near the place where she had died, refused food, and soon afterward was also found dead [of] no discernible physical cause." Simon adds this interesting note: The kind of "true partnership" exemplified by Canada geese, where male and female share all the work of nest-building, rearing, and protecting their young, is "almost always characteristic of species whose sexes look so much alike that it is often impossible to distinguish the male from the female on the basis of appearance."

Speaking of nest-building, the geese are better lovers than architects. Their nest is not a marvel of engineering. The female scratches out a site on the ground (usually), near water, and slightly elevated for good visibility; then the two birds throw the thing together from whatever's available: dry grasses, sedge, lichens, moss, and some down for lining. The occasional nest *not* on the ground is more compelling. One researcher for Bent's *Life Histories* tells of climbing a tree to investigate an osprey nest and finding himself scolded not only by the ospreys but also by a pair of Canada geese. In the same nest he found two eggs from the ospreys and three from the geese.

That's a rarity. These off-the-ground nests have in most cases been *previously* used by hawks or ospreys, but in either case the question arises: When the precocial chicks hatch, how the heck do they get down? One answer comes from *Life Histories* correspondent H. B. Young, on Reelfoot Lake in Tennessee, where the goose family had settled into a nest fifty feet high in a lightning-blasted tree hanging over the water. When the chicks were out of the shell, the gander began swimming around in circles below, hollering and beating the water with his wings, apparently making enough racket to scare away all the catfish, loggerheads, moccasins, eagles, and otters that might otherwise have been interested in the proceedings. With the coast clear, the mother goose pushed her brood one by one down into the water and then followed them, at which point the reunited family quickly paddled to the shore of a secluded cove. (This strategy, I presume, is less successful when the nest is not located over water.)

If a Canada goose's eggs manage to survive, despite the threat of predation by foxes and bears or gulls and jaegers, credit is due to the courage and tenacity of the gander, who protects the nest with testosterone-fueled aggression. "Should he spy a raccoon making its way among the grass," writes Audubon, "he walks up to him undauntedly, hurls a vigorous blow at him, and drives him instantly away." If the threat level is high enough, the gander "urges his mate to fly off, and resolutely remains near the nest until he is assured of her safety." Audubon himself tested the mettle of a particularly stout male when he happened to approach too near a nest. "So daring was this fine fellow, that in two instances he struck me a blow with one of his wings on the right arm, which, for an instant, I thought, was broken."

The devotion of both parents to the young is, for me, fully captured by the image of the goose family's first day on the pond. The proud father leads the way, followed by the file of downy hatchlings one after another, with the mother bringing up the rear. Both male and female, Audubon tells us, remain with their offspring until spring comes around again.

Since these birds are mostly vegetarian, food is plentiful on the summer range for parents and children. Much of it comes from underwater, and the geese don't mind turning their feet and fannies skyward as they pull tender plants from the bottoms of shallow ponds. The young don't need a lot of help; they can dive for food within hours after hatching. A rainy spell might bring some variation to the menu. Audubon says that when the showers are over, the geese "are frequently seen rapidly patting the earth with both feet, as if to force the earth-worms from their burrows."

It seems like a pretty nice life. After a good meal on a peaceful afternoon, the geese enjoy a nap while floating in deep water, swimming slowly in circles with one foot on automatic paddle, or maybe just drifting in the wind. But actually something is happening that makes the goose's life more stressful than it might appear. During their summer molt, they lose their primary wing and tail feathers, so for most of July and into August they are grounded. Now they keep to the marshes at the edge of the pond or, if out on the water, watch nervously for the eagle's shadow. On land during this period, they can play a fine game of possum if the need arises, lying perfectly still with their necks stretched out in front of them. Bent says this stratagem works perfectly on rocky shores, since the bird's rounded gray back looks exactly like a stone. "But sometimes, when surprised," he writes, "the bird's natural cunning fails it. Running to hide, it at times seems to believe that if it can get its head out of sight under some foliage or behind a stump, the rest of its body is likewise invisible."

In most situations, though, Canada geese are wary and intelligent in their own defense. When the flock is roosting, the ganders take turns standing watch. And they know the malevolent from the innocuous. The sight of cattle or horses or deer doesn't perturb them, says Audubon; but the approach of a cougar or a bear "is instantly announced," and at the sound of an Indian's paddle "that may by accident have struck the side of his canoe," every goose in the flock raises its head "to watch in silence the movements of their enemy."

As autumn days turn cooler, the geese take to the sky for their southward migration. The strongest birds share the chore of leading the famous V-formation, "cleaving the air in advance," as Bent puts it, with the others trailing along in the diverging lines, "so spaced that each has room enough to work his wings freely, to see clearly ahead, and to save resistance in the wake of the bird ahead of him." After a hard day's flying, the geese may spot a familiar lake on which to spend the night; they may even be cheered to hear the welcoming call of geese already arrived. But watch out! These supposed cousins may well be "domesticated traitors," trained to lure the migrating flock down toward the hunter's blind.

If such is their fate, they have a lot of company. According to current figures, some 2 million Canada geese are "harvested" every year. We're not to shed tears, though, because we're assured that this species represents one of the great success stories in wildlife management.

Which brings us back to where we started—or to the general neighborhood anyway. Yes, there are now too many Canada geese, it seems, and managers are shifting their focus from conservation to population control as complaints from aggrieved suburbanites rise in volume. Some interesting programs have been initiated: collecting eggs and relocating them to less controversial habitats, inducing flocks to move by manipulating the food supply, and, my favorite, training sheepdogs to herd geese away from prized recreational areas like golf courses.

It seems like a lot of trouble, but what are you going to do? We've despoiled the garden, and now we're doomed to suffer the curse of Adam: of all things under the sun, either too little or too much . . . and the ladies forever likely to ruin their pretty shoes.

·········

American Crow
Corvus brachyrhynchos

The leaves, though still green, are falling from the cherry tree, the air is cooling, and the crows are suddenly loud in the woods. I don't know why. I can't spot the hawk or owl that they might be ganging up on, but, if nothing else, there's a poetic argument for these birds' announcing themselves at the dying of the year. Watching them through my binoculars, I marvel again: The crow is a study in black. Its plumage is black, its bill is black, its eyes are black, its feet are black. The bird is utterly, remarkably black. Natural enough, then, that the crow brings with it the chill of the graveyard at midnight, as well as an enduring reputation for malfeasance. Wasn't it a crow that helped work the witch's will in Disney's *Sleeping Beauty*, crows that led the onslaught in Hitchcock's *The Birds*?

Growing up on my grandfather's farm, I was drilled in the standard anti-crow catechism. They were nuisance birds, to be got rid of by any means. Of course, there are no means by which to get rid of the crow. My grandfather even offered us a quarter a bird for any we could lay at his feet, but I'm sure he knew his money was safe. Only later did I run across the old corn-planting rhyme that expresses the farmer's frustration:

> One for the cutworm
> One for the crow
> One to rot
> And one to grow.

That is, you might as well figure in the crow's take from the get-go.

Most everybody seems to have it in for crows. Farmers hate them for plundering their cornfields, orchards, and chicken yards; hunters hate them for raiding the nests of waterfowl and game birds; "sentimentalists" hate them for eating the eggs and nestlings of their favor-

American Crow (John James Audubon, The Birds of America, vols. 1–4, Special Collections, University Library System, University of Pittsburgh)

ite songbirds. To compound all these sins, says Forbush, the bird rises too early. While the rest of us are still asleep, "the crow is up to some abominable mischief in the back yard."

Not surprisingly, this deep-seated and widespread antipathy has given rise to efforts to destroy the crow that go far beyond my grandfather's small bounty program. The fact is that crows have been murdered by the millions, most effectively through bombing their roosts. A particularly horrific example is reported in *Life Histories*: "Frank S. Davis, inspector for the Illinois State Department of Conservation, killed 328,000 crows in roosts near Rockford, Illinois, with the use of festoons of dynamite bombs. This wholesale slaughter was given great publicity, appearing with photographs in the issue of *Life* for March 25, 1940."

But here's the astounding thing: There are more crows in America now than there were when the first settlers arrived on our shores. From this I infer that the crow, like the cockroach, will still be here when human beings are long gone. Or, to revise Faulkner just slightly, the crow will not merely endure; it will prevail.

How has the crow managed to thrive in the face of all the ill will marshaled against it? Well, in the first place, it will eat anything, and because it will eat anything, it can live anywhere. Sure, farms are great, but so are forests, cities, garbage dumps, and roadsides. Crows like carrion as much as buzzards do, but the bird you see feeding by the highway is more likely to be a crow — because carrion is not its only food. If some idiot litterbug throws a McDonald's sack out the car window, for example, it will be a crow rummaging through it for that last French fry.

The crow will go where the food is — and just eat it all up. Analyses of the crow's diet, populationwide, blunt the force of this truth by suggesting that since it eats a little bit of everything, it doesn't eat too much of anything. For example, in *Life Histories* we learn that, belying its reputation for eating the eggs and young of other birds, the U.S. Biological Survey showed that less than 1 percent of adult crows had such food in their stomachs, and only 1.5 percent of nestlings had been fed such food. But such statistics flatten out the kind of local incident by which the crow earns its black stripes—like in 1940 on the coastal prairie in Texas (as reported in *Life Histories*), when a colony of 1,500 little blue herons and 3,000 snowy egrets was completely destroyed by a flock of 40 crows that ate all the eggs and young. Or those 5 days in 1992 (according to *Birds of North America Online*) during which 2 crows absconded with every single egg—45 from 39 nests—in a least tern colony in Venice Beach, California.

Plus, crows have figured out ways to find food—and get at it—that would leave other birds scratching their topknots. They use their bills expertly, not only to pick at the ground and flick aside nonfood items, but even to grab and turn over larger objects (like dried-up cowpies) to get at whatever might be underneath. They also use their bills to dig into the muck to forage for clams, another favorite food. But how does a crow eat a clam? you might ask. Well, he carries it sufficiently high into the air, spies a nice rock to drop it on and, voilà—clam on the half-shell. This is his method of choice for anything that has a hard shell (turtle hatchlings, nuts of various kinds), except on days when all that flying and dropping just seems like too much trouble. Then, at least according to some crow-watchers, he'll scatter a few nuts in the middle of the road and wait for passing cars to crack them open. All else failing, the crow might fall back on simple thievery. In my favorite instance, cited by Verbeek and Caffrey in *The Birds of North America Online*, a crow pecked the tail of a northern river otter feeding on a fish; when the otter whirled around to chase the crow, a couple of other crows swooped in and stole the fish.

I said earlier that when crows find something to eat, they eat it all up. That's not entirely accurate. For example, when three crows, working at the job for a little over two hours, caught 79 out of 100 white mice released in a field, you're right to assume that they didn't eat all 79 at once. In fact, the ones they didn't eat, they stored for later, another skill they've mastered. As Verbeek and Caffrey report, with extra food to put aside (a bit of fish, a clam, a snake, a frog, a couple of pecans, some corn, whatever), the bird might check out a number of possible cache sites, all the while looking around to make sure no other critter is watching. At the selected site, it digs a hole with its bill, drops the item inside, then covers it up with grass or other plant debris. Since crows eat — and sometimes hide — carrion, the extent to which the hidden food might decompose before the crow gets back to it is presumably not an issue.

Yes, crows are smart birds, maybe the smartest of them all. If you took one from its nest early enough, you'd likely end up with an interesting pet. Citing a couple of earlier sources, Charlotte Green tells one story (from Anna Botsford Comstock) of a pet crow that would steal all the thimbles in the house and bury them in the garden, and another (from A. A. Allen) about a crow that played marbles with his children, learned to talk, and would even seesaw by itself when the children weren't around. *Life Histories* adds that crows are adept at hide-and-seek, especially if it's food that's been hidden, and that they "take delight in shredding the prettiest flower blossoms in the garden." They are also accomplished mimics and, parrotlike, can master a small vocabulary. When talking bores them, they can reproduce a variety of other sounds, like the crying of a child, the squawking of a hen, or a rooster's *cock-a-doodle-doo*.

Maybe the most remarkable and unusual aspect of crow behavior, though, is its social organization. Writers from every era have agreed that crows form an unusually strong nuptial bond and that the mated pair exhibit real affection. Writing for *Life Histories*, for example, Alfred Otto Gross talks about the many times he has seen one of the pair "caress the other with its beak and pick gently at its head [while] the mate would put up her head to be caressed," bringing to mind a pair of billing doves. This apparent devotion led the older writers into the mistaken belief that the male and female work together to incubate the eggs and rear the young. What those writers didn't realize is that crows live in extended families, or "cooperative groups," that typically consist of eight or nine members — including the breeding pair, yearling "helpers" (the pair's children from the year before), and adult helpers (probably the pair's children from preceding years).

Under observation at various sites, these helpers have been seen at virtually every domestic task: hauling in materials for nest-building; taking a turn on the eggs or, more often, bringing food to the mom while she incubates; cleaning the nest; and helping feed the young, both before and after fledging. What makes them do it? Which birds become helpers and which become breeders? Given that crows can live twenty years or longer, will some helpers eventually become breeders and, if so, after how many years of helperhood? According to Verbeek and Caffrey's account, much about this unique behavior remains to be understood, and because they are notoriously hard to capture for banding, the crows don't make it any easier. What's clear is that these birds' social organization is complex, intriguing, and worthy of study.

All the more reason to admire, rather than revile, the crow—if any more reason were needed, that is. Audubon long ago found more than enough virtue in the crow and believed that all efforts toward its destruction were motivated by ignorance. "The Crow devours myriads of grubs every day of the year," he wrote, "that might lay waste the farmer's fields; it destroys quadrupeds innumerable, every one of which is an enemy to his poultry and his flocks. . . . I cannot but wish that they would reflect a little, and become more indulgent toward our poor, humble, harmless, and even most serviceable bird, the Crow."

Maybe Audubon witnessed all the violence visited upon the crow without foreseeing how impervious the bird would prove. Thoreau, writing just a few years later, seemed more sanguine about the crow's prospects: "This bird sees the white man come and the Indian withdraw, but it withdraws not. Its untamed voice is still heard above the tinkling of the forge. It sees a race pass away but it passes not away. It remains to remind us of aboriginal nature."

....

Great Blue Heron
Ardea herodias

Did I see, or did I dream that I saw, in an estuary along Florida's gulf coast, a boy standing motionless, knee-deep in the water, his fishing rod poised in patient stillness, and beside him, not ten feet away, a great blue heron standing equally still, as though it were the boy's familiar? It seems unlikely. The great blue has a reputation for being so skittish that you can't get anywhere near it. "I have seen many so wary," says Audubon, "that, on seeing a man at any distance within half a mile, they would take to wing." That's been my own experience, too, here on Pumpkinvine Creek, where one comes to spend the fall and winter. We see it occasionally, but always after it has seen us, its slow, graceful wingbeats carrying it on down the creek and away.

On the other hand, E. B. White reported that he had discovered he could approach to within about eight feet of a little blue heron simply by entering the water and swimming slowly in its direction. "Apparently he has decided that when I'm in the water, I am without guile — possibly even desirable, like a fish." Granted, the little blue is not so famously wary as the great blue, but maybe this explains what I think I saw in Florida: Maybe that great blue was sizing up the boy for a meal.

The bird is a prodigious eater, after all. Audubon saw one eat "a bucket full of young mullets in half an hour" and guesses that, on average, they consume "several hundreds of small fishes" in a day. True, a boy would be hard to swallow whole, as the heron does a small fish — after tossing it up in the air to get it to come down head-first. But the great blue is not averse to larger game, which it either spears with its beak or grabs between its mandibles, then hauls to shore and beats to death on a rock. Sometimes it spears more than it can handle. Audubon saw one strike a fish that was too heavy to pull up out of the water and that, instead, pulled the heron under and would have drowned it if the bird hadn't finally managed to free itself. Afterward, he says, "it appeared quite overcome, and stood still

144

Great Blue Heron (John James Audubon, The Birds of America, *vols. 1–4, Special Collections, University Library System, University of Pittsburgh)*

near the shore, his head turned from the sea, as if afraid to try another such experiment." So I'm still thinking about that boy.

(The fish-loving heron family, by the way, has devised a number of hunting techniques that go well beyond the great blue's standard "wait-and-stab." Africa's purple heron, for example, steps carefully into the water and straightens its skinny body into one thin line, even the bill pointed upward and the whole figure always inclined toward the sun, so as to make virtually no shadow that might betray its presence. The small black heron takes precisely the opposite tack; it runs along the shore, then freezes and spreads its wings like an umbrella, waiting for a minnow to swim into the shade—though it's unclear whether the minnows actually seek the shade or the heron simply sees better after blocking the sun. But leave it to the green-backed heron, a good old North American species, to exhibit some real yankee ingenuity. This bird has figured out how to pick up bread crumbs from picnic grounds, then drop them in the water as minnow bait.)

When we picture the great blue—"so grand, so majestic, and so picturesque," as Bent describes it—we're likely to be picturing just one, rising from the side of a lake, say, or flying low over coastal marshland. Or, as poet Coleman Barks writes, "stretching between hemlock and laurel, / moving slow against the creekwind." That's the bird we've seen, silent and solitary, a wonder that stops us in our tracks.

Get a crowd of them together, apparently, and the scene is less inspiring. Great blues are colony nesters, and their rookeries, hidden away on swampy islands or hummocks, don't have a lot of tourist appeal. "Dismal retreats," Audubon calls them.

But that's the point for these reclusive birds, who, mindful of predators, take to such secluded spots to build their large, platform-like nests as high in the trees as possible. First-year nests are so thinly latticed that the pair's eggs can be seen from below, but the birds return to the same site year after year, and the nests are built up over time. Not only is more nesting material added, but, as Bent puts it, "the accumulated filth helps to cement the material together." As testimony to the nests' eventual solidity, Bent mentions that a photographer friend of his once sat in one for several hours while taking pictures of birds in nearby nests.

The male and female have mated for the duration of the season, and they share all the chores involved in producing the next generation. They take turns sitting on the eggs, the male on duty for most of the daylight hours, the female working the night shift, and the one not sitting bringing food to the other all the while. Their "mutual affection," says Audubon, is matched by their solicitude for their young, for whom they provide so abundantly "that it is not uncommon to find the nest containing a quantity of fish and other food, some fresh, and some in various stages of putrefaction."

Spare the rod, they say, and spoil the child. As the nestlings grow (four of them, in many cases), the parents' devotion is put to the test. It appears that no amount of food can satisfy their gluttony, no matter how the old birds wear themselves out. Finally, at four weeks, the parents cut back to one feeding a day, as if thinking to teach the kids the virtue of self-denial before sending them out into the world—which, eventually, they do, despite the children's reluctance to get off the dole.

They're gone, finally! But *sheesh*, look at the mess. Bent, noting that the young birds, as they grow bigger, become increasingly "awkward, ungainly, and pugnacious," describes an additional unpleasant habit. "The young instinctively try to void their excrement by squirting it over the edge of the nest, but they are not eminently successful at it and the nest, the tree, and the ground under it are usually completely whitewashed with their profuse ordure before they are fully grown." The mass of decaying fish that has fallen out of the nest makes the place all the more inhospitable, and, according to Bent, the guest who tries his luck can "expect an occasional shower bath from one or both ends of a frightened young heron." Even Audubon quailed at the prospect of investigating a heronry—"the effluvia," as he put it, "being extremely injurious to health."

A messy business all the way around, it seems—just like birthing and raising children elsewhere in the natural order. Maybe this explains why the great blue, after the breeding season is over, again takes up its simple, solitary life. Even the two mated birds go their separate ways, each to find its own haven. Too large to have enemies (except for people, who are not so much a threat to shoot the bird but are always eager to drain its marshes), the great blue passes its days in quiet watchfulness.

The next breeding season will call it back to the chaos of reproduction, but that season, too, will end, and the waning of summer will bring the solitary bird back to Pumpkinvine Creek, or to that peaceful estuary along the gulf coast. The great blue may live for thirty years—an immortal, you might say—enduring the rigors of rookery and child-rearing only so that it might return to its aloof, lonely, but lordly life.

It occurs to me that the one I saw in Florida may well have been much older than the boy beside it, may well have regarded the boy as its familiar. Wise as well as ancient, this bird offers a lesson in right living that Siddhartha would surely endorse: It steps into the stream, gathers itself in perfect stillness, and waits.

·········
Turkey Vulture

Cathartes aura

Hope you don't mind: I prefer "buzzard." Ornithologists will insist that "buzzard" properly refers to the broad-winged hawks of the genus *Buteo*, like the red-tailed and red-shouldered hawks. To this any southern farm boy is likely to reply, "Listen, I know a hawk from a buzzard, and a buzzard is a buzzard." Besides, you know the old expression, "That smells worse than the underside of a buzzard's wing"? Try substituting "turkey vulture." Just doesn't work, does it?

One of the strangest bird encounters we've had here in these woods happened on a gray November afternoon a few years back when we were returning home from somewhere, winding down the driveway, coming around the last bend toward the clearing, and saw buzzards *everywhere.* There were a dozen on the ground in the woods off to the right, others in the leafless trees, and still others swooping and circling overhead. Finally deciding to be disconcerted by my approaching truck, they made a slow retreat to the dead oak tree at the south end of the house, where for an hour they sat perched — thirty-five buzzards hunched forebodingly in that bare, black-limbed tree. An unnerving sight. I looked for but never did see — or smell — whatever it was that lured them in the first place, which surprised me. I was expecting a dead deer, or fawn anyway. I later read that a dead snake is all it takes to bring fifty buzzards down out of the sky.

Talk about a thankless job: to rid the world of carrion, to remove the putrefying filth from roadside, field, and forest. You have to wonder: Would the whole world just *stink* if it weren't for buzzards? At least a little appreciation is intimated in the Latin name, which derives from Greek *kathartes*, meaning "a purifier." In a similar vein, poet David Bottoms pays tribute by describing these birds as "transmogrifying angels."

Otherwise, they don't get a lot of credit. In fact, they inspire such revulsion that they've been persecuted for sins they've never committed — like being a vector of livestock disease. Even cleared of such charges, the buzzard wears forever the cloak of death and the stench

Turkey Vulture (John James Audubon, The Birds of America, vols. 1–4, Special Collections, University Library System, University of Pittsburgh)

of decay, and not without reason. Riding those thermals high in the sky, the buzzard is a beautiful bird, but up close, hulking over a dead and bloated possum on the side of the road, its red head glistening with gore, this bird is hard to love.

In earlier days, evolutionarily speaking, the buzzard was presumably a less ignoble bird, one that at least did its own hunting and killing. It still has the predator's hooked bill, suitable for tearing flesh; but as its diet evolved, so did its feet, and it no longer has either strong legs or useful talons. This explains why you'll see them feeding wherever they find their food, even if it's on the side of a busy highway. Their feet are too weak to carry food away to a location more conducive to pleasant dining. Austin adds that the buzzard's bareheadedness is another feeding adaptation: "The carrion they eat would soon stain and mat down their head feathers."

You notice we've also raised a question that has long occupied buzzard-watchers: Just how do they find that food? Probably because what they ate often stank, it was long assumed that buzzards operated largely out of their sense of smell. But Audubon was already trying to debunk that notion back in the 1830s. In one experiment, he stuffed the skin of a deer with dried grass and positioned it in an open field, legs up and apart as if "dead and putrid." Soon a vulture appeared, alighted, and approached. He jumped on the animal, "raised his tail, and voided freely (as you well know all birds of prey in a wild state generally do before feeding)." He then moved to the eyes (painted clay) and tried to pluck them out to eat. Failing there, he moved to the other end and started tearing at the stitches and pulling out all the stuffing. Finally he gave up and took off, but kept sailing by, "as if loath to abandon so good-looking a prey."

Next, taking the opposite tack, Audubon threw a dead hog into a ravine, concealed it under briars and cane stalks, and let it putrefy. Soon enough the stench was so bad that he himself "could not come within thirty yards of the place"; but the vultures never found it, and eventually, with the help of dogs and other carnivorous mammals, it succumbed to natural decay.

So Audubon concludes that it is by sight that buzzards hunt, and by sight that they communicate their discoveries to one another. "A flock of twenty may easily survey an area of two miles," he writes, "as they go turning in large circles, often intersecting each other in their lines, as if forming a vast chain of rounded links." Eventually, one bird will see a promising meal below and begin to descend; another sees him see it, another sees that one, and so on, until the feeding flock has congregated. What's more, says Audubon, buzzards not only see but *discern* illness or helplessness in potential prey. These birds will wait patiently for the expiration of an old, emaciated ox or a deer mired in the mud of a lakeside, but, he writes, "they frequently pass over a healthy horse, hog, or other animal, lying as if dead, basking in the sunshine, without even altering their course in the least."

A century later, though, the question was still being debated. Winsor Marrett Tyler, contributing to *Life Histories*, objected that experiments where food is hidden might "test the bird's ingenuity [but] do not call for the employment of the faculties with which nature has equipped the bird to use in finding its food." He suspected that the bird's sight and smell were both "very keenly developed" and, stirring the pot again, cited experiments showing that buzzards are sometimes lured to their food by the *sound* of carrion-drawn flies. To sum up, he writes, "The literature to date leaves the reader with the belief that the vulture is a bird not very intelligent from the human standpoint, but alert and keen to detect the presence of food by every sense at its command."

Fair enough, but not the final word. Contemporary researchers, with the tools of modern science at their disposal, have found that while the buzzard makes use of both sight and smell, it does have a more highly developed olfactory system than most other birds of prey, including the condors or the other vultures. Add in anecdotal observations that buzzards have been caught in traps baited with scent only, that they find concealed food by approach from downwind, and that they are attracted to mushrooms and flowers with carrionlike fragrance, and we're back where we began: If it stinks, a buzzard'll be all over it.

But if how they find their food has been a subject for debate, there's never been much argument about what they do when they find it. The only question is how graphically to paint the canvas. Audubon, never squeamish, doesn't disappoint here:

> The accumulated number then fall to work, exhibiting a most disgusting picture of famished cannibals; the strongest driving the weakest, and the latter harassing the former with all the animosity that a disappointed hungry stomach can excite. They are seen jumping off the carcass, reattacking it, entering it, and wrestling for portions partly swallowed by two or more of them, hissing at a furious rate, and clearing every moment their nostrils from the filth that enters there, and stops their breathing. . . . Soon all these bloody feeders are seen standing gorged, and scarcely able to take wing.

Tyler describes the feast offered up by a dead pig on the side of the road: "A bird sails along, doubles back, alights, and, folding its great wings, slowly approaches the pig. With head high and tail held well above the ground, it sidles about, wary and watchful lest the pig move, it seems; then reassured, it steps upon the body and, with a deft hook of its beak, extracts the eyeball and swallows it." So much for hors d'oeuvres. Then the bird moves down and makes its first incision over the upper part of the shoulder blade, pulling the skin back to expose the muscles. "The vulture at its meal moves deliberately," writes Tyler, "but, like a skilled workman, surely."

Forbush begins with the moment the first bird begins to descend from its high, circling search. "It may be that its keen eyes have spied a dead or dying animal, or a corpse rising to the surface of a stream, or even the village toper fallen by the wayside." Soon every buzzard for miles around has gathered for the feast, alighting first on trees or fences. "A few of the boldest drop to the ground," Forbush continues, "and with exceeding circumspection approach the object of their quest." Once assured that the animal in question is, in fact, dead, and with their appetites fully aroused . . . but here Forbush is restrained by civility. "Over what follows," he writes, "let us draw the veil."

Thankfully, turning to the courtship behavior of the buzzard brings a pleasanter picture into focus. In the spring we might find eight or ten together, males and females, assembled on a fallen log. Like shy teens at a mixer, they begin to pair off couple by couple. Audubon pictures each pair flying off from the others, "alone and in love" and "sailing side by side the whole day." The truth is odder, and maybe even more romantic. Paired buzzards enjoy a lengthy honeymoon, sitting together at their chosen nest site for days or even weeks before laying begins.

Buzzards also mate for life, and, although they don't go to a lot of trouble to build a nest, the two parents fully share in the monthlong incubation of the two eggs the female has laid in a hollow tree. Unfortunately, the eggs must eventually hatch, and then we have, well, buzzards. We know the parents' feet are too weak to carry food back to the nest, so the babies are fed by regurgitation. A lot of birds do that, of course, but buzzards do it with special vehemence. *Life Histories* describes a scene with the young chick's bill thrust deep into the mother's gullet, and "the feeding process carried on so vigorously that it resembled a tussle, both birds swaying their heads up and down and from side to side and balancing themselves by raising their wings."

What's more, the young spend an unusually long time in the nest, two months or more—another mark of the parents' devotion when you consider all the regurgitation and defecation that goes on. Leave it to Audubon to point out that "their nests become so fetid, before the final departure of the young birds, that a person forced to remain there half an hour would be in danger of suffocation." This means you, committed buzzard researcher. If you get too close to the nest, the hatchling will only add to the mess by instinctively throwing up the throw-up it has just fed on.

Not even other predators can love a buzzard. If its foul-smelling vomit fails to thwart an attack, its second line of defense is to play dead—which, needless to say, would make it of interest only to another buzzard.

Frankly, the list of this bird's unsavory habits has not yet been exhausted, but enough is enough. In fairness, we should close by thinking again of the great work undertaken by these "purifiers," these "transmogrifying angels," who, in Bottoms's words,

> flock to the side of the poisoned fox, the mud turtle
> crushed on the shoulder of the road,
> who pray over the leaf-graves of the anonymous lost,
> with mercy enough to consume us all and give us wings.

White-Breasted Nuthatch

Sitta carolinensis

Thomas Burleigh assigns the white-breasted nuthatch to Georgia's "mountain counties" and says it's "noticeably scarcer" throughout the Piedmont. Charles Seabrook, the *Atlanta Journal-Constitution*'s nature columnist, agrees that the brown-headed nuthatch is the more common member of the family in our area here around Atlanta. But my birds didn't get the word. I see the white-breasted almost exclusively, and I see it all the time. The explanation, I think, is that the brown-headed has a thing for pinecone seeds, while my mostly deciduous woods offer fine habitat for the white-breasted, whose diet is more wide ranging and who likes decay-softened hardwoods for nesting as well. Now, especially, with the cherry tree almost bare and a good many other species checking their passports, these hard-working, sunflower-seed-loving birds are conspicuous.

Not that I have anything against the brown-head (which I do see on rare occasions), but I do believe that the white-breasted is the handsomer bird—formally attired in gray cutaway, white shirt, and—for the male at least—black top hat. (The crown of the female is gray, an easy distinction between the sexes). It also occurs to me that the dignity of his attire suggests a standard of living to which this bird strives mightily to conform. Austin calls him an "earnest little bird," and Tyler, writing for *Life Histories*, elaborates on the point: "He has none of the irrepressible fidgetiness of the house wren, none of the charming happiness of the song sparrow; he appears to take life on a matter-of-fact level." Moreover, when we see him in his characteristic posture—working his way headfirst down the trunk of a tree, his face out at a ninety-degree angle, and looking, frankly, a bit silly—we understand that the nuthatch's journey toward middle-class respectability will be a difficult one.

He does try his best, though. In fact, his ingenious feeding routine happened to be one of the first interesting bits of bird behavior I ever noticed. Like the titmice and chickadees, the nuthatch takes a sunflower seed from the feeder and flies off with it. But while the others

White-Breasted Nuthatch (John James Audubon, The Birds of America, vols. 1–4, Special Collections, University Library System, University of Pittsburgh)

typically alight on a limb and hold the seed down with their feet while they break it open, it looked to me like the nuthatch preferred to wedge it into the deeply cut bark of a sourwood tree and then have a go at it. It turns out I wasn't the first to notice this procedure. "Their bill is strong and sharp," wrote Audubon way back when, "and they not unfrequently break acorns, chestnuts, etc., by placing them in the crevices of the bark of trees . . . where they are seen hammering at them for a considerable time. The same spot is usually resorted to by the Nuthatch as soon as it has proved to be a good and convenient one." Presumably, the feet so well adapted for climbing up and down tree trunks are less well suited for holding a nut or seed in place.

Sometimes, though, the bird wedges the comestible into its crevice and leaves it there, for the nuthatch, ever seeking to secure its station in life, is one of our provident, food-storing birds. All their favorite nuts and seeds—including sunflower seeds from the feeder—are hidden away, to be used, as Forbush says, "in time of want when ice storms coat the trees, if the jays and squirrels have not already stolen them." But the prudent nuthatch will not be done in by marauding jays. This bird is careful to "scatterhoard" its largesse, industriously distributing food all over its territory and using each secret spot for only a single food item.

Tyler adds suet to the list of cached food and reports that one male was observed digging out pea-sized pieces, then flying off in all directions, for up to a hundred yards, to find his various hiding places. When his mate showed up, Tyler continues, he enlisted her aid, placing the morsels in her bill and sending her off. The telling detail from this anecdote, though, is that while the male was happy to dole out to his mate the pieces he had extracted, he absolutely forbade her from getting at the main store. And who can blame the thrifty, cautious burgher? Clearly, a prodigal spouse could prove as ruinous to his chances as predatory jays and squirrels.

Yet, like any bourgeois householder, the nuthatch is a devoted husband and father. Courtship begins in late winter, with the male's attempt to woo the female with song. Consistent with his sober demeanor, however, the nuthatch is no musician, and his love song sounds not too different from the nasal, workaday *quank-quank* every-one is familiar with. It's simply speeded up and intensified, something like *ank-ank-ank-ank-ank-ank*. He is on safer ground when he begins to bring her food, which, of course, he has set by in abundance. For-bush writes that the "gallant and attentive" male "even shells seeds for her and passes her the freed kernels."

For their nest, they like to find a decayed, easy-to-excavate spot in the trunk or branch of an old deciduous tree, or they might find an already-made cavity, maybe a woodpecker's former home. Once the site has been selected, the female does most of the work, but the male makes himself useful by bringing in nesting material or food or whatever else she might require. As Audubon puts it, "The male, ever conspicuous on such occasions, works some, and carries off the slen-der chips, chiseled by the female. He struts around her, peeps into the hole, chirrups at intervals, or hovers about her on the wing."

The pair raise a large family — as many as eight or ten young — and continue to care for them for two or three weeks after they leave the nest. Eventually, as summer turns to fall, the young must leave to establish their own territory, and for the mated pair, who will remain together after the children have gone, it's back to work.

Does the nuthatch loaf like the dove or play "pass the flower petal" like the waxwing? No. This bird seems to understand that evolution had a reason for supplying it with its long, powerful bill and that to fail to use it would constitute a crime against the natural order of things. So there it is, all the livelong day, scouring the tree trunks up and down, down and up. That kind of foraging, of course, is for the summertime insects and larvae, which the nuthatch discovers and devours without discrimination. (They're even said to enjoy tent caterpillars, but I'm bound to mention that they were not in evidence when the tents in my cherry tree could have used policing.) When the insects become scarce, the nuts are ripening, and then, as we've noted, the nuthatch only redoubles his effort. Autumn, as Keats per-sonifies her, might be found "sitting careless on a granary floor," but the nuthatch is busy feeding today and providing for tomorrow.

Such is the life of the decent, circumspect, and straightlaced nuthatch, at least as I've observed it. Admittedly, it's been noted that there's a sociable side to the bird's nature, that it seems at times to take pleasure in the presence of humankind and has been known to come when whistled for and alight on the hand or shoulder of people with whom it has become familiar. I haven't witnessed any such thing myself.

In fact, I'm thinking it's not a matter of sociability. According to *The Folklore of Birds*, the Cherokees called this bird *tsuliena*, meaning "deaf," because it so tolerated the presence of people that it seemed deaf to human noise and activity. Now that I understand. Toiling 24/7 like an avian Ebenezer Scrooge, this stolid citizen wouldn't look up from his work even if Christmas bells were pealing.

Bald Eagle
Haliaeetus leucocephalus

I saw a bald eagle once. It was on a still-warm autumn morning six years ago, and I was in a boat on the Little St. Marks River, a beautiful little stream that runs off the Apalachicola near its mouth on the Florida panhandle. It flew low across the river and was gone quicker than we could look at each other and say, "Did you see that?" Twenty-five years earlier I probably wouldn't have seen one. A century earlier I might've seen a dozen or so.

The fish-loving bald eagle (or, translating the scientific name loosely, the "white-headed sea eagle") was so abundant in the early twentieth century that the folks in Alaska got worried about their salmon population and, in 1917, started offering a fifty-cent-per-bird bounty. By the time the program was outlawed by the feds in 1952, the price had gone up to two dollars a bird and more than 128,000 bounties had been paid out. The intentional slaughter (of which the Alaska bounty program was only part) together with the unintentional destruction of the species caused by DDT and other pesticides had, by 1966, brought the once-plentiful bird under the protection of the Endangered Species Preservation Act and, subsequently, under the Endangered Species Act of 1973. The ban on DDT and heightened environmental consciousness more generally have helped reverse the decline, and the bald eagle population has been slowly increasing since 1980.

The restoration of this majestic bird, whose population had plummeted to some 500 breeding pairs, total, by 1963, is a cause for celebration—and rightly considered one of America's great conservation triumphs. The bald eagle came off the "endangered" list in 1995, to the delight of ornithologists, naturalists, and birders everywhere. I've got to say, though, with my glass of champagne in one hand, it's very weird to hold in the other the classic writings about the bald eagle that date from before its existence was threatened. In fact, reading what the masters had to say about the bald eagle is akin to reading what Noam Chomsky has to say about U.S. foreign policy—that is, eye-opening.

Audubon, for example, describes the bald eagle as a bird of "ferocious, overbearing, and tyrannical temper" and offers this typically graphic hunting scene from the shores of the Mississippi: The male is on one side of the river, "perched, in an erect attitude, on the highest summit of the tallest tree," and his mate is similarly situated on the other side. While they wait for promising quarry, she "warns him by a cry to continue patient." He answers "in tones not unlike the laugh of a maniac."

They ignore all manner of waterfowl whose rapid flight or aerial skill might prove too challenging. They're waiting for the ungainly swan, which soon enough comes flapping laboriously up the river. The eagle starts from his perch "with an awful scream, that to the Swan's ear brings more terror than the report of the large duck-gun." The swan would love to plunge into the river to save itself, but the eagle is familiar with this stratagem and "forces it to remain in the air by attempting to strike it with his talons from beneath." Once the eagle has forced the wounded swan to the ground, "then, reader, you may see the cruel spirit of this dreaded enemy of the feathered race." Driving his claws deep into the breast of the swan, he "shrieks with delight, as he feels the last convulsions of his prey." His mate "now sails to the spot where he eagerly awaits her, and when she has arrived, they together turn the breast of the luckless Swan upwards, and gorge themselves with gore."

With the coming of the osprey in spring and summer, the eagle exhibits an even more ignoble hunting tactic. When the skilled fisher-bird rises from the water with its hard-won supper, the eagle, "like a selfish oppressor," drops down from above with talons outstretched. Unable to defend itself while holding onto its meal, the osprey must let go of the fish, which the eagle swoops down on and carries away.

Worst of all, says Audubon, the bald eagle is a carrion-eater, happy to devour "the putrid flesh of carcasses of every description," even if it has to drive away the buzzards to do so. In one "ludicrous instance,"

Bald Eagle (John James Audubon, The Birds of America, *vols. 1–4,*
Special Collections, University Library System, University of Pittsburgh)

he writes, an eagle came upon a flock of vultures devouring a dead
horse. At the sight of the eagle, the vultures took off, one of them
trailing a "portion of the entrails, partly swallowed" from his beak.
"The Eagle instantly marked him, and gave chase. The poor vulture
tried in vain to disgorge, when the Eagle, coming up, seized the loose
end of the gut, and dragged the bird along for twenty or thirty yards,
much against its will, until both fell to the ground, when the Eagle
struck the vulture, and in a few moments killed it, after which he
swallowed the delicious morsel."

Audubon not only agrees with Benjamin Franklin that the bald
eagle should never have been selected as our national emblem; he
quotes the letter in which Franklin voiced the famous opinion:

For my part, I wish the Bald Eagle had not been chosen as the representative of our country. He is a bird of bad moral character; he does not get his living honestly; you may have seen him perched on some dead tree, where, too lazy to fish for himself, he watches the labour of the Fishing-Hawk; and when that diligent bird has at length taken a fish, and is bearing it to his nest for the support of his mate and young ones, the Bald Eagle pursues him, and takes it from him. . . . Besides, he is a rank coward: the little King Bird, not bigger than a Sparrow, attacks him boldly, and drives him out of the district. He is, therefore, by no means a proper emblem for the brave and honest Cincinnati of America, who have driven all the King Birds from our country; though exactly fit for that order of knights which the French call Chevaliers d'Industrie.*

Arthur Bent also begrudges the bald eagle its place of honor. He calls it "a fine *looking* bird, but one hardly worthy of the distinction. Its carrion-feeding habits, its timid and cowardly behavior, and its predatory attacks on the smaller and weaker osprey hardly inspire respect and certainly do not exemplify the best in American character." But he can't bring himself to go along with Franklin's preference for the wild turkey: "Such a vain and pompous fowl would have been a worse choice." Besides, says Bent, with its "soaring flight, with its pure-white head and tail glistening in the sunlight," the bald eagle "may still be admired by those who are not familiar with its habits."

Bent, though, is one of those who *are* familiar with the bald eagle's habits, and he lays them out there. For example, though perfectly capable of catching a duck on the wing, the eagle would rather pounce upon the poor bird in the water, forcing it to dive again and again "until it becomes exhausted and is easily captured." If the duck doesn't tire quickly enough, the eagle will call on his mate for help.

---

*"Cincinnati," as Franklin uses it here, is presumably the plural form of Cincinnatus, the Roman statesman of the fifth century BC. Thus the phrase might be read as "the brave and honest statesmen of America." "Chevaliers d'Industrie" may be translated simply as "swindlers."

About its nest, says Bent, the eagle is "an arrant coward," immediately fleeing at the approach of an intruder and squealing in protest from a safe distance. And speaking of squealing, Bent describes the voice of the bald eagle as "ridiculously weak and insignificant . . . quite unbecoming a bird of its size and strength." If you think that by this point Bent has rendered the poor eagle sufficiently "ridiculous," you are wrong. Even the female's eggs, he says, are "ridiculously small."

Forbush is more sympathetic, writing that while the bald eagle "may deserve some of the epithets that have been heaped upon him, . . . nevertheless he is a powerful and noble bird and a master of the air." Just as he defends the blue jay, Forbush suggests that the eagle has simply learned to do what it needs to do. If there's not a hard-working osprey handy, or any already-dead fish, he will certainly catch his own, a task to which he brings great skill. And who wouldn't love to witness the eagle's acrobatic "kill maneuver," where he sweeps underneath, turns upside down, and sinks his talons into the breast of his quarry?

Forbush also points out that, from the agricultural point of view, the eagle is harmless. It doesn't eat fruit or grain and, except in very rare instances, leaves the farmer's chickens alone. And as for its appetite for carrion, what's wrong with keeping the shorelines cleaned of dead fish? Forbush was also aware, even before midcentury, that the bald eagle's numbers were declining, and he wasn't happy about it. This bird, he writes, "should be rigorously protected at all times by law and public sentiment to save it, if possible, from extirpation."

Fifty years later, he's getting his wish, and I, for one, will sing halleluiah. The good folks at the Department of Natural Resources tell us that bald eagle nests (eight feet across, some of them, and weighing as much as a ton) on Georgia's Lake Seminole are again productive, and that the number of hatchlings has been gradually increasing since Georgia's eagle population began to be tracked in 1988. Naturalists here and elsewhere can rest easy knowing that they'll be able to watch the regal adult pairs, mated for life, conscientiously raise their one or two young over the six-month-long breeding season, and they will be able to study those young during their own five-year journey toward adulthood—only at the end of which will they earn their own white head and tail feathers.

That's wonderful news, and no one (not Audubon or even Franklin) would say otherwise. But wouldn't it have been interesting to have lived in those days of yore when species like the bald eagle weren't threatened and weren't protected either—when they just *were*. When Audubon could see literally hundreds of bald eagles on one of his trips down the Mississippi, or (even a century later) when Bent could write that the species was "very common for a large bird" and that it frequently nested near houses, along busy roads, and even on golf courses.

It occurs to me that it may be easier to attribute humanlike faults and failings—cruelty, cowardice, tyranny—to the wild creatures whose populations, like our own, teem relentlessly.

Great Horned Owl
Bubo virginianus

Barred Owl
Strix varia

Dede and I were on the front porch a little later than usual one evening this past October. The air was so perfectly pleasant we hated to come inside, so we sat there and let the dark come down. Suddenly, from very close by, right at the edge of the woods, we heard a scream that jerked us bolt upright. Best we could tell, somebody had just been murdered not thirty yards away.

I've since deduced that what we heard was the scream of the great horned owl, which Charlotte Green calls "one of the most bloodcurdling sounds heard in the woods." Sometimes females scream in defense of their nest, but no great horned owls were nesting within spitting distance of our house. More likely it was a youngster, just a few months out of the nest, who hadn't quite figured out the territory thing yet and didn't know any better than to just holler. In any case, it's not something you'd want to hear if you were camping out in the middle of the wilderness.

The great horned is one of North America's biggest, fiercest owls. It's not common in our woods, and we feel fortunate to have seen it even once — in the almost-gone light of a November evening, when one lit for a moment on the limb of an oak behind the house, then was gone again on silent wing. More often we just hear its eerie call — something that might be rendered *hoo-hu-hoo, hooo, hooo*. It's almost exclusively nocturnal, which makes its reputation as a predator all the more macabre. As Forbush puts it, "Every living thing above ground in the woods on winter nights pays tribute to the Great Horned Owl except the larger mammals and man." It terrorizes the farmyard as well as the forest, killing not only the ducks and chickens but also the geese and turkeys, despite their much greater size. Where it finds its favorite birds roosting in the trees, it sometimes plays the role of

Great Horned Owl (John James Audubon, The Birds of America, *vols. 1–4, Special Collections, University Library System, University of Pittsburgh)*

ghoulish stalker—alighting beside its prey and crowding it off the limb, only to strike it dead in midair.

It appears to have a special fondness for rabbits, but virtually any small mammal will do—weasels, minks, voles, moles, squirrels, rats, and even skunks. With its appetite for this last item, as Burleigh points out, it begins to redeem itself, "for skunks are notorious predators upon ground-nesting birds, and, except for the Great Horned Owl, have almost no enemies." But its murderous nature reasserts itself: When prey is plentiful, it kills wantonly and eats only its victims' brains.

The bird is eerily equipped for success as a nighttime marauder. Like all owls, it has excellent night vision, but perhaps even better hearing. That round, flat facial disc in which owls' eyes are set is a remarkable receptor of sound waves, which it funnels into the ear openings, located under feathers beside the eyes. (Those feather tufts on the heads of this and the other "eared" owls are not ears, by the way. They probably serve as camouflage, by breaking up the bird's otherwise conspicuously round-headed outline.) What's more, because the owl's flight feathers have a soft, downy fringe—rather than being stiff to the tips—the bird can fly, and even take off, in absolute silence. So, there you are, minding your own business (in the middle of the woods on a dark night). You can't see it. You can't hear it. Before you know what happened, it's all over you like a cheap suit.

If you think you've got a great horned nesting in your neighborhood and want to investigate, be on the lookout—or listen-out—in late fall and early winter. Mating season comes with the New Year, and here in the South the female might even find eggs in her nest for Christmas. It's during this season that you're most likely to hear them, but seeing them is another matter. They're adept at staying out of sight during daylight hours, and even if you find the nest, you might not know it. It'll be too high up to see what's inside it, and, since owls don't like to build their own nests, it may well be one you saw a family of hawks in the winter before. Forbush says the best way to find one during the day is to follow the clamor of a pack of angry crows.

Of course, you might want to try during the night when the birds are active. And you might get lucky. On the other hand, the female, who defends her nest aggressively, might just light on a branch right over your head and let out that horror-movie scream, in which case you'll probably just wet your pants and run for home.

THE BARRED OWL IS A LITTLE SMALLER and considerably less savage than the great horned, but no less vocal. You've probably heard the distinctive hooting—*hoo hoo huh-hooo, hoo hoo huh-hoo-awwww*—often rendered as "Who cooks for you, who cooks for you-all." Maybe you've heard what Bent calls "the antiphonal hootings of a pair of these owls," calling back and forth to each other through the darkened wood.

But have you heard the bizarre caterwauling a party of these owls will set up during the mating season? Bird writers can't resist trying to describe these cacophonous nocturnes. Forbush recalls nights made hideous by the owls' "grotesque love-making" as they utter "the most weird and uncouth sounds imaginable." Audubon says the owls' "discordant screams" are "so strange and ludicrous" as to be compared to "affected bursts of laughter."

Dede and I have heard it often, and as far as mating rituals go, it's about as terrifying and hilarious as you can imagine—sort of like drunk fraternity boys on a midnight sorority-house raid.

Its disconcerting vocalizations aside, the barred is a kinder, gentler owl, at least compared with the great horned. Audubon accuses it of being "a great destroyer of poultry, particularly of chickens when half-grown," but later writers haven't supported this claim. Bent calls it a "decidedly beneficial species," thanks to its fondness for rats, mice, and other rodents. On the other hand, he admits that the barred will sometimes eat other birds, including smaller owls, and he adds the interesting observation that if you have barred owls in your woods, you won't have screech owls, or at least you won't hear them screech.*

---

*Our own experience would seem to bear out this theory. We've never heard a screech owl in these woods, and what a pity. To me the screech owl sounds exactly like a horse

Barred Owl (John James Audubon, The Birds of America, vols. 1–4,
Special Collections, University Library System, University of Pittsburgh)

Barred owls are also more common than great horned owls, and less exclusively nocturnal, which gives you a better chance of catching a glimpse of one — maybe gliding low over a field in the late afternoon, looking to snatch up a mouse. But wait — don't owls see poorly during the day? Audubon helped perpetrate this misconception when he wrote that the barred owl's daytime vision "seems to be rather of an equivocal character." He explained he "once saw one alight on the back of a cow, which it left so suddenly afterwards, when the cow moved, as to prove to me that it had mistaken the object on which it had perched for something else." Much as I love that story, I have to take the word of Bent and all subsequent writers that owls generally have excellent vision, whether day or night. (On the other hand, owls are singularly unable to move their eyes within their sockets, an inability they compensate for by being able to turn their necks well past 180 degrees in order to see in any direction.)

Even if you catch sight of one, though, you'd still need luck to find a nest, since this owl prefers to make its home in a hollow tree. Where such quarters are not available, the barred, like the great horned, is likely to appropriate a previously used hawk's nest. If the pair can't find a good one, these architecturally challenged birds will settle for a poor one and make no effort to improve it. In a worst-case, last-resort scenario, they might try to build their own, but the cobbled-together affair will be so insecure that the eggs are likely to roll out or fall through.

If you happen to find an owl "pellet" on the ground, chances are you're standing below not the nesting nest but the feeding nest. Like

---

whinnying — which is a mighty weird noise coming out of the trees in the middle of the night. But it was Thoreau who immortalized the call of this bird. "Wise midnight hags!" he called them. "It is no honest and blunt tu-whit tu-whoo of the poets, but without jesting, a most solemn graveyard ditty, the mutual consolations of suicide lovers remembering the pangs and the delights of supernal love in the infernal groves. . . . *Oh-o-o-o-o that I never had been bor-r-r-r-n!* sighs one on this side of the pond, and circles with the restlessness of despair to some new perch on the gray oaks."

other large owls, and hawks, too, barred owls like to have a place to carry their prey to, tear it up, and eat it in comfort. Since they gulp it down without chewing, they swallow a lot of indigestible parts — bones, fur, feathers, and so forth — which, before they can eat again, they have to cough back up (or "cast") in a compact mass about the size of a sweet-gum ball. Specialists, of course, can break these things apart and tell exactly what the owl had for dinner — like the sample I read about that contained the skull of a ruffed grouse. How interesting it would be to find such an odd piece of skeleton *and* be able to identify it. I don't know about you, but I wouldn't know the skull of a grouse from the skull of a mouse.

Barred owls, like other members of the family, are long lived, monogamous, and highly territorial. Utterly nonmigratory, they hold onto and defend their large home range not only during the breeding season but throughout the year and into succeeding years. So it's possible for me to imagine that we have been listening to the same pair of barred owls (and their generations of children) throughout the dozen years we've lived in these woods.

In a time of suburban sprawl, heedless development, and vanishing habitat, I confess to taking comfort in the thought — and pride, too, though I don't really deserve it.

PERHAPS NO BIRD FIGURES MORE PROMINENTLY in myth and legend than the owl. From time immemorial its nocturnal predation and haunting songs have made it an omen of death or other tidings of woe. Yet it has an equally long history as a symbol of wisdom, whether as the familiar of the goddess Athena or perched on the shoulder of the magician Merlin in the days of King Arthur.

One hopes that this reputation for wisdom explains why, today, the owl is the mascot of no fewer than thirteen U.S. colleges and universities, including bastions of learning like Bryn Mawr, Rice, Temple, and Kennesaw State University (where Dede happens to teach). But — especially caught up as we are in another football season — one realizes that such hope is in vain. In most of these cases (as at KSU, where the mascot's feather tufts suggest the bloody-minded great horned owl), the adjective "fighting" generally precedes "owl" in sideline cheers and athletic slogans.

To my knowledge, and to my chagrin, no student cheering section in this great nation of ours has ever stood up and hollered, "GO YOU THINKING OWLS!"

"Confusing Fall Warblers"

With the exception of the pine warbler, which we'll return to, the warblers don't come to me, so I decided to get out of my armchair and go to them. It was fall migration time, and the warblers (along with a good many other species) pass over nearby Kennesaw Mountain; so when brother Richard called to say he was heading out there early on a Saturday morning, I figured it was time to break the rules and "go birding."

By the time I got there at eight, Richard had already introduced himself to a trio from Athens, who appeared to know what they were doing and who didn't seem to mind if we tagged along. First, in a sort of a warm-up exercise, they led us down a short service road bordered by a forest of oak and hickory dense with brushy understory. Immediately we saw a hooded warbler, a striking little bird whose bright yellow face shines through a black cowl that completely covers its head and neck; it was, of course, a first for me. I thought, *Well, this ain't half bad*.

Then, along with a few other scattered groups of birders and innumerable walkers and joggers, we followed the main road that leads to the mountaintop. The going up and coming back down took about four hours, but it turns out my day had been made at 8:15. I *might* have caught a glimpse of a bird that *might* have been a chestnut-sided warbler, but the hooded was the only warbler I know I saw.

Not that the rest of the day was lost. Other birders did better than I, and birder-watching, too, is pretty good sport. The leader of our little group, a portly, genial, and generous-spirited man, seldom lifted his binoculars to his eyes. He just listened and checked the species off in the little notebook he carried. At one point he told us we were listening to a yellow-throated vireo. I told him it sounded so much like the red-eyed vireo that sings in my woods all summer long that I didn't believe I'd be able to tell the difference.

"Sure you can," he said. "Hear how this one sounds a little bit hoarse?"

Oh, okay.

I also enjoyed listening to our group exchange notes with the others we met. "Seen anything?" "Got a Tennessee, and I'm pretty sure we got a Maggie." Nobody had seen a cerulean, apparently the great prize, but one birder explained that they had already come through earlier in the month. One group reported seeing a flock of a dozen or so scarlet tanagers, which, I have to say, would have been pretty cool.

Otherwise, the young woman in the group from Athens pointed out a Cooper's hawk hunting in the underbrush; Richard caught sight of—or claimed he caught sight of—a female redstart; and, most oddly, from the very mountaintop, we saw an osprey circling lazily high in the sky.

I thought I might try one more time. I showed up a few days later for an officially guided tour led by the Atlanta Audubon Society's Chuck Saleeby. Chuck was great. He saw warblers everywhere: "There's a Tennessee. There's a Blackburnian. There's a chestnut-sided. There's a black-throated blue." Sometimes I got my glasses trained in the right vicinity in time to catch a glimpse of one of the little varmints hopping around in the foliage. But which one was it? Chuck—and everyone else—had moved on.

I need to go again. And again. And again. In the company of an expert who can devote all of his or her attention to *moi*. Or I can throw in the towel, settle back in my armchair, and—*ahhhhhh!*—prop up my exhausted feet.

I MENTIONED THAT THE CERULEAN (*Dendroica cerulean*, or "sky-blue tree-dweller") is the great trophy of warbler hunters. That's not only because it's such a beautiful little bird, but also because it's getting harder and harder to spot. As Charles Seabrook reported a few years back in an *Atlanta Journal-Constitution* series called "Georgia's Disappearing Songbirds," the cerulean's population has plummeted 70 percent in the past thirty years. Consequently, the tiny, brilliant-blue bird has become emblematic of the perils faced by so many of our neotropical migrants and, in a larger sense, of the great pitched battle: *Homo sapiens v. Omnia altera.*

In the spring, when the cerulean returns from Central America (where habitat loss is already causing enough problems), it seeks out nest sites in mature hardwood forests with tall trees and relatively few saplings and shrubbery. Call the bird picky if you want to, but it hates to breed in tracts of woods of fewer than 500 acres and really prefers unbroken expanses of several thousand acres. Not too many years ago, of course, such tracts were everywhere. Now, thanks to development of every sort—reservoirs and river diversion, highways and power lines, housing and industry—they're being broken apart. As Brent Martin, director of Georgia Forest Watch, told Seabrook, "The only place where ceruleans still nest in Georgia is in the northwest corner of the state. But development is gobbling up everything between Atlanta and Chattanooga, and the bird doesn't stand a chance."

The question is, Which of our neotropicals will survive? Seabrook points out that dozens of our eastern songbirds are struggling against serious population declines and that the cerulean is far from the only one in dire straits. The gorgeous painted bunting has lost half its numbers; the wood thrush is down by 40 percent.

Habitat loss is the greatest problem by far, but by no means the only one. Seabrook writes that telecommunication towers, skyscrapers, and other high-rise structures kill 100 million migrating birds every year—the vast majority of which are our neotropical songbirds. But we need our telecommunication towers—don't we?—just like we need houses and roads. Maybe we don't need songbirds, although without them we'd surely have a plague of insects that would destroy the trees even before the loggers could get at them.

It's a problem, isn't it? For me the solution seems obvious: drastically fewer people. Not that I'm volunteering.

AT LEAST ONE WARBLER SPECIES, thankfully, has less to fear from the hazards of migration: *Dendroica pinus*, the pine warbler. Forgive me for sounding possessive, but this is *my* warbler, the one I see, recognize, and listen to all fall and winter, the one who, despite the preponderance of hardwoods in my forest, makes himself a familiar

visitor at my seed and suet feeders and relieves, somewhat, the guilt I feel at knowing so little about his extended family.

I don't have to trudge up Kennesaw Mountain to see migrating pine warblers because many members of this species live all year long in the pine woods of the Southeast. While some of its numbers may breed up North, their southward migration at the end of the season might well come to its terminus right here in my little piece of forest. Burleigh describes the pine warbler as "one of the more plainly colored members of the genus *Dendroica*," and I suppose that's true. But as autumn leaves turn brown and fall away, as the goldfinches fade to gray, and as the gray and black of the nuthatches and chickadees blend into the gray landscape of bare limb and tree trunk, the pretty yellow breast of the pine warbler is a mighty welcome sight.

I never see or hear this bird after the weather warms up in the spring, but that may not mean it doesn't nest here. During the warm months, it will find plenty of insects to eat and won't need to come to my feeders. Plus, even if it were breeding here, I'd be very unlikely ever to see the nest, situated, as it is, high up in a pine tree and, as Harrison puts it, "completely hidden from below in a cluster of fine needles." I'd like to, though; it's said to be particularly comfy, a compact cup warmly lined with fur and feathers. Apparently this bird is as industrious as the titmouse in collecting nesting materials. Burleigh reports that one female was seen "gathering nesting material from the side of a crow's nest that held eggs but from which the owner was temporarily absent; and another observed a few days later was busily engaged in lining her nest with bunches of fur plucked from a dead cat lying in an open field."

I say I don't hear it during the summer, but maybe I'm not listening. According to Audubon, "It sings at all hours of the day, even in the heat of summer noon, when the woodland songsters are usually silent." Or maybe, in fact, it doesn't breed here and only arrives in my

Pine Warbler (John James Audubon, The Birds of America, vols. 1–4,
Special Collections, University Library System, University of Pittsburgh)

woods to spend the off-season. In any case, when I do hear its soft, sweet, musical trill, I'm delighted—and reassured to know that I'll have this lovely bird to keep me company during the coming winter.

If one warbler is all I get, then this one—"the gentle, modest minstrel of the pines," as Forbush calls it—will suit me just fine.

Winter

Sandhill Crane

Grus Canadensis

A few notes from my journal:

> February 8, 1999: Outside planting a couple of nandina, heard the gabbling of migrating sandhill cranes. Looked up to see two long Vs flying over, the second circling overhead long enough for me to grab my nocs off the porch and get a good look—feathery wing-tips, long necks, long legs straight out behind. Way high in a glary sky. Mary Hood says you can call them down, but you'd have to holler mighty loud. . . . February 9, 2001: The sky filled with sand-hill cranes, circling and gabbling, heading, it seemed, generally north, high in the sky. . . . February 12, 2003: Mild day, beautiful deep blue sky, sandhill cranes overhead. . . . February 10, 2006: Two long Vs over the golf course, northward bound.

I believe I discern a migratory pattern. Back in the 1930s, Bent speculated that the Florida cranes were permanent residents and that the migrating birds headed down to Louisiana, Texas, and Mexico, rather than to Florida. More recent information from *The Birds of North America Online* assures me that I haven't been hallucinating all these years. It turns out that the ones I see represent the "Eastern Greater" subspecies, which breed in Michigan, Minnesota, Wisconsin, and Ontario and migrate through Illinois, Indiana, Ohio, Tennessee, Kentucky, and Georgia to winter in southern Georgia and central Florida. Their major migration stopover (in case you want a look) is the Jasper-Pulaski Fish and Wildlife Area in northwestern Indiana. They leave their nesting grounds in early October, and the stopover peak occurs in late October. They arrive in southern Georgia and Florida from mid-November to mid-December. They're not supposed to head back north until late February or early March, so I guess the ones I see every year are the fidgety, type-A birds that can't wait any longer.

In any case, it's a wonderful sight, and maybe a more wonderful sound. You always hear them before you see them, and sometimes

Sandhill Crane (John James Audubon, The Birds of America, *vols. 1–4,*
Special Collections, University Library System, University of Pittsburgh)

(especially if you're old and don't have your glasses on) you might not see them at all. They've been known to fly two miles high. You notice I call their sound "gabbling," but that may not be very close. "Honking" is wrong. Canada geese honk. Best of all might be this description from one of Bent's experts, Hamilton Laing: "It is a hoarse, unnatural croak that rips from the throat, a vibrant puttering that seems to suggest something prehistoric — such a call as one might expect that our far-gone ancestors heard in the days when pterodactyls and their kind flew about the marshes." Then again, as one old legend has it, maybe the birds are saying "corpse, corpse, corpse," foretelling a death to come to the house they are flying over.

Cranes are one of the ancient bird families. "A very old group," wrote Austin in 1960, "barely able to maintain themselves" and in trouble everywhere except in some Buddhist countries, "where they are protected by religious beliefs and by superstition." Trouble was visited especially upon the whooping crane, whose numbers had declined, as of 1941, to fewer than two dozen individuals. But thanks to a recovery effort initially launched by the Audubon Society and subsequently taken up by wildlife organizations throughout the United States and Canada, fifty years later the whooper's population, counting both captive and wild birds, was back up to 257. Not a huge number, granted, but at least no longer on the brink of extinction.

The situation was never quite so dire for the sandhill, though Bent laments that "the advances of civilization, the drainage of swamps and the cultivation of prairies have doubtless driven this wary, old prairie scout away from all the central portions of the United States, and are still driving it farther west and north into the unsettled wilderness." The cranes need wetlands, both for breeding and along their migratory routes. Experts today tell us that fewer than twenty salt lakes in West Texas provide roost areas for up to 80 percent of the midcontinent population during winter. Those same numbers take refuge in the "wet meadows" of the North Platte and Platte River valleys in Nebraska during their spring migration. Their survival, obviously, depends on the protection of such habitats.

If you're an armchair birder like me, you probably won't get to the

Platte River valley or to the Jasper-Pulaski Fish and Wildlife Area in Indiana. If you did, though, you'd get to see some pretty spectacular bird behavior: the cranes' famous "dancing ceremony." It begins with the birds walking around one another with quick steps, their wings half spread. Suddenly they leap into the air, sometimes fifteen or twenty feet high, their legs held below them straight as a gymnast's; then they float back down to earth. In between leaps they bow and stretch gracefully, or, for a special encore, they pick up pieces of grass in their beaks, throw them up in the air, and stab at them as they come back down. The ceremony is assumed to be a part of courtship during mating season, but the odd thing is that the birds do it all year long—an expression, some believe, of their generally exuberant nature. *The Birds of North America Online* has broken the dance down into its five basic "moves": the upright wing stretch, the bow, the vertical leap, the vertical toss, and the horizontal head pump, which brings to mind kids at a hip-hop concert.

Sandhills like to nest in shallow marsh ponds, surrounded by water, where they pile up an island of dead reeds and rushes, sometimes four feet across. Both sexes go at this task, picking up nesting material from the immediate vicinity and tossing it over their shoulder until they've built up a big enough mound. Then one of them, usually the female, hops on top and starts arranging it to form a depression in the middle. Here she will lay her two eggs, but it's a Cain-and-Abel story. The precocial young engage is such a fierce sibling rivalry to establish dominance that, often, only one will survive.

Except for their inability to prevent this conflict, though, the sandhills are excellent parents. Both incubate the eggs (the male even developing a brood patch for the purpose), and the young, whether one or two, are nurtured in the family bosom until the following spring rolls around. As a testimony to parental devotion, Bent tells the story of a young crane, wounded by a hunter and unable to stay airborne in its attempt to escape, whose parent flew underneath it, "and with its feet settled on the adult's back, bore it off to safety."

After their year at home, the young move in with others their age, the so-called subadult/nonbreeder flock. As the cranes are particularly long-lived birds, this period of freedom and irresponsibility may last for several years (a behavior pattern my own generation exemplified to a spectacular degree). Not until the age of six or seven have a substantial majority of the young birds paired off. Meanwhile, their faithful parents, mated for life, continue to raise ever-younger sisters and brothers. In fact, the cranes' longevity and fidelity have won them a place in ancient myth. Austin writes that "in Japanese folklore the crane is supposed to live a thousand years, the turtle ten thousand. Both these animals are frequently used as symbols for a long and happy life in birth and wedding ceremonies, the crane frequently perched on the turtle's back."

In calling these birds "wary, old prairie scouts," Bent means to be taken literally. "First to the feeding ground at dawn go the scouts, the wise ones," he writes; ". . . the others follow when the coast has been declared safe. In feeding, the several units scatter widely; every unit has one or more scouts on high-headed guard; eyes are pointed at every angle, and approach by a foe is almost impossible." Apparently, the wariness was evident even before their prairie marshes began to disappear. "The acuteness of their sight and hearing is quite wonderful," wrote Audubon in the 1830s. "They generally see you long before you perceive them," and by the time you have perceived them, they're gone. "For my part," Audubon continues, "I would as soon undertake to catch a deer by fair running, as to shoot a Sand-hill Crane that had observed me."

If wariness fails, these birds fall back on sheer aggression. On one of his trips down the Mississippi, Audubon shot a sandhill crane on a sandbar, then set his gun down in the boat to go fetch it. But the bird was merely wounded, and seeing him coming, it ran away "with the speed of an ostrich" and would have escaped if Audubon hadn't cornered it against a pile of driftwood. As Audubon approached, the bird turned on him, raised up to its full height, shook its feathers defiantly, "and advanced upon me with open bill." Exhausted from the chase, Audubon was not up to the confrontation and began to back away. The bird continued to advance — "until at length I fairly turned my back to him, and took to my heels, retreating with fully more speed than I had pursued. He followed, and I was glad to reach the river, into which I plunged up to the neck, calling out to my boatmen." There they remained, Audubon neck-deep in the water and the crane holding him there, until the boatmen came up for the rescue, "and highly delighted they were with my situation."

Contemporary crane-watchers would not discredit this account. According to the literature, while any number of predators—foxes, raccoons, coyotes, wolves, bobcats, crows, ravens, eagles, and owls— feed on the eggs or the young or the sick or injured adults, healthy adult sandhills can take care of themselves. When threatened from above, the crane vaults into the air toward the potential predator, throwing its feet forward in a vicious kick. When confronted by an animal (not excluding the human species) on the ground, the initial response is the "spread-wing posture," with the open bill thrust out— as in, "You want some of this?" If you think you might want some, the bird comes at you with a hiss and a stab, followed, for good measure, by one of those lethal jump-kicks. I believe I'd take to the river, too.

Or better yet, I'll stay here in the yard and put some fresh mulch around those nandina, the winter sun warm on my back. Alert, though, and hopeful that those high-flying sandhills will be on schedule, their throaty call rippling across the sky, telling me that February is nigh half-gone and spring is on the way.

....

Blue Jay
Cyanocitta cristata

Three or four blue jays passed through one day in late January, splashing a little color (*cyanos*, Greek for "blue") onto the bare branches of the cherry tree. It was a welcome but unusual sight. Fact is, I don't see many jays here in my woods. The reason, I believe, is that they've all moved to town, where the living is easy and where there are plenty of house cats to torment.

Loud and abrasive even on its best days, hollering out its onomatopoeic *jeer, jeer*, the blue jay has plenty of detractors, none more vehement than Audubon. "Who could imagine," he writes, "that a form so graceful, arrayed by nature in a garb so resplendent, should harbour so much mischief—that selfishness, duplicity, and malice should form the moral accompaniments of so much physical perfection!" They rob the farmer of his newly planted corn, says Audubon, of his peas and his sweet potatoes; while they're at it, they "attack every fruit tree," and once they've wiped out the fruit and vegetable produce, they go after the eggs of the farmer's chickens.

For any jurors still unpersuaded, Audubon tells the story of the slaughter of all the birds in the Charleston aviary. At first, rats were suspected, but no one could discover how the big rodents might have got inside the place. It seemed unlikely that mice could be doing the damage, but they were rounded up and put to the sword just in case. "Still the birds were killed, from the smaller to the larger, up to the Key-West Pigeons." Finally the identity of "the depredator" came to light: a jay that had been raised in the aviary. The bird's true character was revealed when he was captured and placed in a cage, along with some corn, some flour, and a few of the small birds he had already killed. "The birds he soon devoured," writes Audubon, "but the flour he would not condescend to eat, and refusing every other kind of food soon died."

It's true that blue jays can sometimes be an annoyance to the farmer, and also true that during the season they'll sometimes pilfer the eggs or young from the nests of smaller birds. Such unsavory prac-

189

tices may have been the origin of the old superstition—documented
in Martha Young's *Plantation Bird Legends*—that jays are never seen
on Friday because on that day they visit the devil, carrying a splinter
so that "Old Scratch" will have plenty of kindling for his fire.

But while the jay is basically omnivorous, its reputation as a "depredator" has apparently been overblown by sentimentalists. Dependable Professor Beal has reported the facts. In his careful examination of 292 blue jay stomachs, remains of birds were found in
only 2, and the shells of birds' eggs in only 3. His conclusion is that
"the most striking point in the study of the food of the blue jay is the
discrepancy between the testimony of field observers concerning the
bird's nest-robbing proclivities and the results of stomach examinations. The accusations of eating eggs and young birds are certainly
not sustained." In fact, the "animal" portion of the jay's diet (which
is, after all, only one-fourth of the total) consists largely of destructive
pests like grasshoppers, caterpillars, scale insects, and weevils, and
the bird's "economic status" is entirely favorable.

What's more, the blue jay's favorite vegetable food, by far, comes
from the forest, not the farm. In its passion for acorns and other
wild nuts, a more interesting aspect of the bird's character comes to
light—its intelligence. The jay is one of the bird world's great experts
in the useful skill of storing food away for lean times to come. Where
it finds a plentiful supply, the jay might harvest five or six acorns at
a time (two or three in the throat and esophagus, two or three more
in mouth and bill tip), then carry them to a caching site and arrange
them in a pile. One by one it'll bury them, all within a radius of a
couple of yards, then cover each one with a dead leaf or a pebble.
Contemporary observations of six radio-transmitter-equipped birds
showed that each one cached between 3,000 and 5,000 acorns in a
single fall season. While there's no way to track exactly how many of
these nuts are recovered, the worst that can be said is that the un-
recovered ones provide a boon to reforestation efforts. What's more,

*Blue Jay (John James Audubon, The Birds of America, vols. 1–4, Special
Collections, University Library System, University of Pittsburgh)*

the jay's intent is clear; it only caches food in locales where it is a year-round resident. Where it is a summer resident only, *why bother?*

One of Bent's correspondents, W. L. McAtee, reported on what he believed to be another interesting feeding behavior. Watching a jay plucking large ants out of an anthill, he noticed that the bird was picking them up in its bill and then tucking them beneath a raised wing, apparently "taking advantage of the instinct of ants when disturbed to fasten their jaws onto any object that presents itself." The only question in the man's mind was whether the jay was storing the ants for its own later consumption or hauling them back home to feed the family.

What this observer did not realize back in 1946, and what, for that matter, even Arthur Bent did not realize, is that the jay was not feeding; it was "anting"—that is, using ants to clean parasites from its wings. According to *The Birds of North America Online*, the jay's method is to grasp the ant by its head or thorax and direct it abdomen-first toward the underside of its flight feathers, beginning at the base of the shaft and proceeding toward the tip. The ants, in self-defense, secrete their noxious formic acid, and the tiny vermin apparently fall away in a swoon. Once the ant has done its work, the jay removes it (only occasionally eating it) and takes up another one. A single sequence might last a few seconds or maybe a minute; a complete "anting" session might go on for forty-five minutes, perhaps to be followed by some preening and a refreshing bath.

The blue jay's considerable ability as a mimic is sometimes held up as yet another of its attainments. It can perfectly imitate, for example, both the long scream of the red-tailed hawk and the shorter cries of the red-shouldered and sparrow hawks. The question is why. One theory is that the jay is simply an "idiot mimic." It can make the sound, so it does—like a child amusing itself by making the noise of, say, a police siren. Another theory is that the jay screams like a hawk to warn the local population of a hawk's presence—which shows, if not great intelligence, at least purpose. More intriguing is the possibility that the jay uses imitation as a means of deception. As we might guess, this is the theory favored by Audubon, who writes that the jay "imitates the cry of the Sparrow Hawk so perfectly, that the little birds in the neighbourhood hurry into the thick coverts, to avoid what they believe to be the attack of that marauder. [Then the jay] robs every nest it can find, sucks the eggs like the crow, or tears to pieces and devours the young birds." More Audubonian overstatement perhaps, but there are plenty of contemporary reports of the jay's so-called kleptoparasitism—for example, giving the "hawk call" to frighten the grackle, or some other dupe, into dropping its food.

Still, however remarkable its abilities, the blue jay seems fixed in the popular mind as the schoolyard bully who, once punched in the nose, goes crying home to Mama. A mob of jays will delight in harrying the drowsing owl from tree to tree, for example, with nary a one ever coming close enough to risk a feather. "He is more tyrannical than brave," writes Audubon, "and, like most boasters, domineers over the feeble, dreads the strong, and flies even from his equals." It is a fact that, at the feeding station, the bossy jays get the worst of it from a surprising number of presumably less aggressive residents— red-bellied woodpeckers, grackles, doves, mockingbirds, and cardinals, to name a few. They are "always exceedingly garrulous," adds the exceedingly censorious Audubon, "unless a hawk happen to pass suddenly near them, when they are instantly struck dumb, and, as if ever conscious of deserving punishment, either remain motionless for a while, or sneak off silently into the closest thickets."

But even its harshest critic will have to admit that the domestic life of the blue jay is a model of rectitude. Preparing for the brood to come, the blue jay pair almost always build a new nest each year, and they construct it carefully. They pass over the desiccated twigs and sticks they might easily pick up off the ground in favor of fresh, strong wood straight from the tree. The male, who collects most of the materials, will fly a great distance to find freshly dug earth—in the local graveyard maybe—where he can harvest the fine rootlets his mate prefers for nest lining. Civilized city jays like to decorate their nests with factory-made goods—paper, cloth, string, wool, or even those plastic "six-pack yokes," which, maybe thinking to raise property values throughout the neighborhood, they sometimes hang on a branch outside the nest.

Throughout incubation and brooding, which is the work of the female, the male bird dependably provides for both wife and children, but, in fact, his devotion has long since been in evidence. He was bringing treats to his "special friend" as early as Valentine's Day, and since that time the pair have been seen "nudging," kissing, and passing their favorite twigs back and forth. When the moment comes, the female sidles up to the male on their perch and validates the popular idiom by "shaking a tail feather." (Well, her tail begins quivering as she crouches horizontal on the branch.) The male accepts the invitation by mounting her for a second or two, beating his wings for balance during their quick consummation. It may not seem like much, but it works. Blue jays mate for life, and only the death of one of the birds will break the pair's bond.

To me, such constancy is more than enough to restore the reputation of the blue jay, if it needed restoring. Maybe it doesn't; maybe all this talk about the blue jay's character and personality is out of line. After all, of the jay's "so-called cannibalism," Forbush says that "it is his natural prerogative to eat the eggs and young of smaller birds or even the adults in case of necessity, if he can catch them." His right to do so is no different from "that of the little birds to eat flies or caterpillars." As for his habit of "stealing" the farmer's corn, well, "he does not know the grain is not his. It is only when judged by human standards that we find him lacking in virtue."

Finally, though, whether or not the jay is deemed to be "lacking in virtue" is, for me, beside the point. Because what the bird certainly doesn't lack is color, conspicuously missing from my world on these gray winter mornings. To the small company that brightened, for a few minutes, my January morning, I can only say, *Come back, please, whatever your business. And make all the noise you want to.*

....
Bobwhite
Colinus virginianus

Bob WHITE! Poor Bob WHITE! That popular rendering of the bob-white's whistle makes a lot of sense when you realize that it's not, after all, the call of the cock to his nesting mate but, rather, the blue note of the unmated male who has somehow missed out and who contemplates a long summer of loneliness.

Not that you're likely to hear it at your feeder, unless your feeder happens to hang in the middle of a gone-to-seed grain field way out in the countryside. No, the bobwhite quail (or, to translate its Latin name, "the partridge of Virginia") is our classic game bird, the plump little morsel in pursuit of which corporate titans have bought up entire counties in southern Georgia and northern Florida and made them over into quail-hunting "plantations"—complete with the lavishly appointed "big house," pens of highly trained bird dogs, the standard equipage of a hunt wagon pulled by a team of mules, and a whole lot of, well, people on hand to keep the rich folks happy and the whole thing humming. The tradition was effectively mocked by Tom Wolfe in *A Man in Full*, where the wealthy Atlanta developer/ plantation owner tells his guests he hopes they enjoy their supper because, he figures, each one of those quail they're eating cost him about $2,500.

I went on a quail hunt once, a few years back. I didn't feel like "a man in full"—or even "a man in part." Mostly I felt silly. I felt silly when "Old Sam," the hunt master who had been leading these expeditions for a couple of hundred years, immediately reprimanded me for holding my gun pointing groundward instead of skyward. I felt silly when, with too many of us to all fit comfortably in the wagon, I volunteered to ride one of the horses and when, quickly realizing that I had not been on one of his brethren in thirty years or so, the horse vetoed my every command for the next four hours. And at dinner that night, at the long, linen-covered dining room table, when the cook's helper served the soup one person at a time, returning to the kitchen for each bowl, I felt the silly impulse to jump up and help.

Northern Bobwhite (John James Audubon, The Birds of America, *vols. 1–4, Special Collections, University Library System, University of Pittsburgh)*

I also felt silly that I knew so little about our quarry. I knew what everybody knows — that quail, like our other gallinaceous birds, live, feed, and nest mostly on the ground. Having grown up in the country, I had seen the mother and her chicks, in their characteristic single file, crossing dirt roads or skedaddling from the clacking blades of the oncoming hay mower. On the other hand, I hadn't realized, especially after seeing them explode from their coveys and instantly disappear, that quail are actually very poor flyers — at least over the long haul. In *Life Histories,* Bent writes that they would really rather travel on foot, even in their mini-migrations from one feeding area to another, and that if they happen to come to a river and have to fly across, they might not make it. They even "prefer to escape from their enemies by running," he writes, and "a bird dog will often trail a running bevy for a long distance."

Of course, I knew nothing about the domestic relations of the bobwhite. In a scenario unusual in birddom, a month or six weeks might pass between the pairing of male and female and actual nesting. Throughout this period the male follows the female around like a lovesick schoolboy, and, in fact, he remains a devoted husband — except in one circumstance, wherein he illustrates that some men can only take so much domesticity. If called upon to take a turn at incubation, writes one of Bent's experts, "he appears to lose interest in the opposite sex."

Winter is the season of the hunt on these southern Georgia plantations. I believe I was there in early February. We weren't likely to stumble across any nests. A couple of months later, if we had been diligent and lucky, we might have found one. The surprising number of eggs — a dozen or more, maybe even so many that the mother has arranged them in two layers — would have told us what we had discovered. Maybe Old Sam would have cautioned us to leave them alone, heeding the old-time wisdom that a mother quail will abandon eggs that have been handled or disturbed.

When the time is right, the young bobwhite hatches out of its shell with the help of its egg-tooth, a bony little protuberance on top of its bill that atrophies a few days after its purpose has been fulfilled. Forbush writes that after making its initial crack, the hatchling then perforates a line all the way around so that the shell separates as if it had been cut in two with a knife, "and the struggling little chick pops out into the world." Like other wild fowl, quail are precocial; that is, they're ready to get up and go pretty much as soon as they hatch. ("Precocious," obviously, is the human equivalent.) In fact, the little quail are so eager to have at it that you might see one running off with half the shell still stuck to its back.

But if you're on a quail hunt in February, you don't get to see any of this. You do get to observe some aspects of quail behavior, though. You for sure get to appreciate that these birds are masters of camouflage. This is a talent learned early on, since chicks a day or two old are utterly vulnerable to predators, if predators can find them. In our case, we had dogs to find the birds, and of course the dogs operate by smell, not sight. It went something like this: The two pointers ranged far and wide through the broom sedge and wiregrass, Old Sam hollering out their instructions—*"Ro-ah, whooee, hey, ro-ah"*—in a language decipherable only to them. Periodically, not often by any means, one would come to a sudden halt, and the wagon would roll to a stop. If it wasn't just a "kennel point" (a bathroom break), Old Sam, a gunner at each flank, would slowly approach, then whip the tangle of brush where the dog was pointing.

Understand: Nobody ever sees the quail in hiding—not Sam, not the dogs, not nobody. Nobody is absolutely sure they're there until the whip comes down close enough and they explode from the covey in that sudden thunder of wingbeat and flashing feather. In that instant you're supposed to shoot them, and if you miss, too bad. Once the covey has flown and the "scent has been broken," you'll spend a lifetime before you find an individual bird. Not even the dogs can help you then. Some frustrated hunters claim that the single birds have the ability to "withhold their scent," but Bent, for one, doubts any intentionality. It's more likely, he writes, that "the rapid passage through the air dissipates most of the scent from the plumage; the birds, being frightened, crouch low on the ground with feathers closely pressed against the body, shutting in body odors; and as they have not run any there is no foot scent."

The fact that you go out twice a day (even if you might feel once was plenty) points to another interesting facet of bobwhite behavior: They have remarkably regular feeding habits. After the sun has begun to dry the dew from the grass, they head to the nearby stubble field and feed for a couple of hours. Then they take a lengthy siesta, long enough to digest; enjoy a nice dust bath; preen; and catch a nap. About two hours before sunset they return to their feeding grounds for another meal, then call it a day. Bent says that the predictability of this pattern gives the hunter "an unusual advantage," but our party, if it had one, made poor use of it. (Not that Bent claims it's easy: "The man who can put two quail in his pocket for every four shells fired is a good shot," he writes. If you quadruple those odds—one quail for every eight shots fired—you'll get closer to our ratio.)

The hunters give up as the light begins to fade, but the bobwhite have other worries, so they roost in a tight circle, with their bodies packed close together and their heads facing outward. One of Bent's correspondents—watching, not hunting—got to observe the formation of such a circle and noted that when it was complete, two birds were left out. "One stepped up to the group," wrote Dr. Lynds Jones, "made an opening, then crowded himself in, with much ruffling of feathers. One remained outside, with no room anywhere to get in. He, too, ran up to the circle of heads, then round and round, trying here and there in vain; it was a solid mass. Nothing daunted, he nimbly jumped upon the line of backs pressed into a nearly smooth surface, felt here and there for a yielding spot, began wedging himself between two brothers, slipped lower and lower, and finally became one of the bristling heads."

Sadly, even this 360-degree vigilance often comes up short. Bobwhite—adults, chicks, and eggs—are preyed upon mercilessly by hawks, owls, and crows and, on the ground, by raccoons, possums, skunks, foxes, and stray cats (which, says Bent, "should be shot on sight"). Throw in habitat destruction from high-density forestry and "clean farming," which kills all the weeds that supply much of the quail's seed-eating diet, and you've got a tough, short life. Recent studies show that the individual bobwhite, on average, lives less than one year, and, in the bigger picture, populations are declining steadily, especially in the rapidly developing Southeast.

I didn't know any of that, and, anyway, we were on a quail preserve, a managed plantation. So we fired away, relentlessly if for the most part futilely. Somehow, at the end of the day, shooting blindly into the noise of the rising covey, I actually hit one, and the Boykin spaniel trained for the purpose "brought him dead." I held it limp and lifeless in the palm of my hand—a pretty little thing, close up like that, and exquisitely soft to the touch. Then I felt *really* silly.

....

Pileated Woodpecker
Dryocopus pileatus

Like any good southern horticulturist, Don Hastings has a couple of magnificent magnolias bordering the lawn of his beautiful old homestead in Cherokee County, about an hour due east of where I live. Shortly after we Yows had moved to our little piece of country, he invited me over to take a walk through his woods. It was early winter, and his idea was that we would "root prune" some of the magnolia saplings that proliferated throughout his mostly pine forest. I couldn't believe there were so many — or understand why.

"Pileated woodpeckers," said Don. "They're crazy about the seeds that pop out of the fruit cones."

We selected about a dozen that looked promising, four or five feet high, sound and straight-growing, and proceeded to work our way around the root system with a spade, cutting away the root ends in such a way as to leave a manageable root ball. A couple of months later, with the roots presumably scarred over and the air still cold enough for the trees to withstand transplanting, we went back and dug up the trees. Twelve years later (constituting my one and only landscaping triumph) they're flourishing along my driveway and at the borders of my little yard. A year ago the two or three largest of them began producing their gorgeous, aromatic white flowers. It can't be too much longer, can it, before I stumble across the first little seedling in my own welcoming woods.

I've got the pileateds, I know that much. That wonderfully raucous cry ricochets through the woods even if the birds themselves do their best to stay hidden. At all times a shy bird, writes Audubon, "when followed it always alights on the tallest branches or trunks of trees, and removes to the side farthest off, from which it every moment peeps, as it watches your progress in silence." But if they're reclusive, they're also nonmigratory, and the mated pair (who wed for life, by

Pileated Woodpecker (John James Audubon, The Birds of America, vols. 1–4, Special Collections, University Library System, University of Pittsburgh)

the way) are ready at every season of the year to defend their territory with a holler or a drumroll. This means that, for me, anyway, these striking birds are more conspicuous in winter after the leaves have fallen. Looking through my binoculars from my upstairs office window, I can watch them work over the fallen logs or rip the bark from dead pine trees looking for winter sustenance.

They'll find it, too. Their ability to detect the presence of wood-boring beetles or, their special favorite, carpenter ants is uncanny—even in trees with no visible sign of ant damage. "Doubtless that strong formic smell," writes Bent, "coupled with his experience in sounding tree trunks—as a man tells a ripe watermelon by the *plunk* of it—enables him not only to find the tree, but, what is more remarkable, to drive his hole with such precision that he taps the heart of the community." Once the bird has opened up the mother lode, it uses its long, barbed tongue, coated with sticky saliva, to draw out the delectable morsels. Ever marveled at the vast horde of ants that come streaming out of a disturbed hill or colony? No problem for the pileated. According to Professor Beal, as many as 2,600 ants have been found in a single stomach.

More generally, bird writers unanimously agree that the food habits of this woodpecker are entirely beneficial. All of its food comes from the forest, and, in Bent's words, "all its work in the forest helps to conserve the timber." The thing is, though, just about everything this hard-working bird does is admirable.

Like woodpeckers generally, *Dryocopus* (or "tree-cleaver") is a cavity-nester. Pileateds like to excavate their nest holes in tall dead pine trees, with both birds going at it for the better part of a month. (Charlotte Green says the female does most of this work, but recent studies show the opposite is true). In either case, the birds hammer away until a mound of chips has piled up in the cavity, then they take a few moments to throw the chips out one bill full at a time. At first you can see the bird perched on the trunk; after a few days it will have its head inside and its tail sticking out. When the bird is out of sight, you can figure the nest is pretty close to finished.

But this is a bird whose work is never done. In the first place, late the following winter, they'll be excavating all over again, because they refuse to nest in the same cavity twice. What's more, pileateds like to have a different cavity for roosting purposes, and they often excavate two or more of these, perhaps to have an extra in case the first one is discovered by a predator. All this digging can't be easy, but it is to the benefit of the whole forest ecosystem. A variety of other birds—to say nothing of mammals, reptiles, amphibians, and invertebrates—use the pileated's cavities for shelter and nesting.

The pileated pair are excellent parents as well. Once the female has laid her four eggs, the two birds take turns during the eighteen-day incubation period. "It is said," writes Green, "that when one bird wishes to leave the nest it will call the other, and then wait until it comes." Actually, the bird away from the nest, perhaps anxious to take its turn, is more often the one that gives the call; but in any case it is a well-coordinated effort, and current studies from *The Birds of North America Online* have shown that the eggs are attended 99 percent of the time. The male is an unusually devoted father. During both incubation and the eight or ten days of brooding that follow, he splits the daytime duty with his mate but takes over completely at night. Even after the chicks fledge, he and his mate remain on the job, and all through the long summer the family stays close. Only when the young have fully demonstrated their ability to take care of themselves are they encouraged to strike out on their own.

Then the trees in my predominantly hardwood forest take on their autumn reds and golds, and the mated pair are alone again. I'll see them when the leaves fall, flying from ravine to ridge crest, their wild, aboriginal call marking their flight. Burleigh must have had that pulse-quickening cry in mind when he wrote, "To my mind no bird is more symbolical of the primitive wilderness areas than is the Pileated Woodpecker."

Along the same lines, Audubon observed back in his day that the pileateds' "natural wildness never leaves them," and then, to illustrate, he told the oddest story. It seems that the Reverend John Bachman of Charleston took five pileated hatchlings from a nest and tried to raise them in captivity. Three died quickly, and the other two survived only because they were force-fed a steady diet of grasshoppers. Even then, "their whole employment consisted in attempting to escape from their prison, regularly demolishing one every two days," until Bachman substituted oak bars for pine. Every morning after their drink of water, they turned over the saucer. They repeatedly tried to destroy the trough that held their food. Nevertheless, and despite their being "uncleanly and unsociable birds," Bachman kept them until winter. Finally, as he entered his study one morning, one of the birds flew past him, out the door, and into the branches of a nearby apple tree. Inside the study, the other bird was hammering away at Bachman's books. They had finally broken free of their cage and, writes Bachman, "must have been at liberty for some hours, judging by the mischief they had done." The good reverend had at last had enough. He reopened the door leading outside, "and this last one hearing the voice of his brother, flew towards him and alighted in the same tree."

I understand that times have changed, that students of bird life today have means of observing birds in the wild that weren't available to Bachman. Still, those birds wanted out, and I believe I would have gotten the message a little quicker than he did.

Then again, maybe Bachman didn't realize all the critical work these birds are born to do—like devouring noxious carpenter ants, drilling comfy nest and roost cavities, and, not least important, seeding the southern woods with magnolia trees.

AS FOR THE PILEATED'S MAJESTIC COUSIN, the ivory-billed woodpecker, the question persists: Is it hanging on in the swamps of southeastern Arkansas, or has it vanished from the earth?

If you are reading these words, you were probably as excited as birders and conservationists everywhere at the news, in April 2004, that a team of researchers had spotted an ivory-bill in Arkansas's Cache River National Wildlife Refuge. Their best evidence of the sighting was four seconds of grainy video that purported to capture the magnificent bird flying from its perch on the far side of a tupelo tree and disappearing into the swamp. (Trying to navigate the Web to find this video — following a link here, installing and downloading there, backing up and trying again — I was the armchair incarnation of David Luneau, the photographer who shot the footage, paddling his canoe through those pathless waters. Except that I was ultimately unsuccessful.)

The story lost some of its luster a year later when three respected ornithologists claimed the evidence of the sighting to be inconclusive. They didn't question the veracity of the research team, which was, after all, led by the Cornell Lab of Ornithology; they simply weren't convinced that the bird in question was an ivory-bill rather than a pileated.

At the end of the subsequent search season — November 2005 to April 2006 — the Cornell team returned from the field disappointed but not discouraged. They had failed to bring home the "definitive visual documentation" they had hoped for, but they remained convinced that the 2004 sighting was the real thing and determined to continue the search. As Cornell Lab director John Fitzpatrick put it, "The vastness of the forest combined with the highly mobile nature of the bird warrant additional searching."

I wish Fitzpatrick and his team every success, but however his search turns out, the story of the ivory-bill is interesting and instructive.

It's interesting, particularly, to hear Audubon evoke a world long gone when he talks about "frequently observing" the ivory-bill during his travels down the Mississippi River corridor. Interesting, too, that even then, in the early 1800s, he was already pondering the bird's declining numbers. He ascribed the decline to the ivory-bill's unceasing call note — *pait, pait, pait* (now more typically rendered as *kent, kent, kent*) — "heard so frequently as to induce me to say that the bird spends few minutes of the day without uttering them, and this circumstance leads to its destruction." The bird was killed, he explained, for its rare beauty — specifically because "its rich scalp attached to the upper mandible forms an ornament for the war-dress of most of our Indians, or for the shot-pouch of our squatters and hunters, by all of whom the bird is shot merely for that purpose."

Of course, when it comes to the decimation of wildlife species, Indians and hunters and squatters didn't know squat (though it's possible to speculate that the squatters' grandchildren were quick learners). A century later, in 1939, Bent wrote, "Today [the ivory-bill] is almost extinct . . . and has been exterminated from all but a few isolated localities in Louisiana, Florida, and South Carolina, where it still clings on in a precarious position." Trophy hunting was no longer viewed as the principal cause of the bird's disappearance, however, but rather "the destruction of its natural habitat, the virgin cypress and bottomland forests of the South."

As the song says, "That's the way you do it." From Bent's time to the present, we've continued to refine and perfect our instruments of habitat destruction—then whistled blithely as those instruments drove animal and plant species to extinction.

Wait a minute. Wait a minute. Didn't the Bush administration use the reported ivory-bill sighting to promote its "cooperative conservation" program? Didn't it offer $13 million to landowners in the region's flood-plains for habitat protection and maintenance? Isn't that just one example among hundreds? Haven't we turned the corner in terms of environmental awareness?

Hmmm.

American Robin
Turdus migratorius

Linnaeus didn't need to take a lot of poetic license to name the robin "migrating thrush." Spectacular robin migrations have long been part of North American bird lore—like this one documented by venerable North Carolina bird writer Charlotte Green: "Five years ago [1928] the greatest migratory flock of robins ever known was seen near New Hope, Gaston County, North Carolina. Game Warden Ford estimated that there were several millions roosting in the pine woods. For over a week they wheeled about in the sky, coming to rest in the woods, and in flight they appeared like dark clouds. This great flock was the nearest approach of modern times to the flocks of passenger pigeons which, only a few generations ago, were so numerous that they darkened the earth during their migratory flights."

(The common name, by the way, comes from the European robin, familiar in the gardens, hedgerows, and farmyards of Europe and the British Isles. The story goes that the English were so fond of their robin that they took the name along wherever they sailed and gave it to any foreign species that reminded them of their homeland bird.)

A century earlier than Green, Audubon observes that when the vast numbers of robins begin to arrive in the South to spend the winter, "one cannot walk in any direction without meeting several of them." He goes on to say that their arrival "is productive of a sort of jubilee among the gunners, and the havoc made among them with bows and arrows, blowpipes, guns, and traps of different sorts, is wonderful. Every gunner brings them home by bagfuls, and the markets are supplied with them at a very cheap rate. Several persons may at this season stand round the foot of a tree loaded with berries, and shoot the greater part of the day, so fast do the flocks of Robins succeed each other. They are then fat and juicy, and afford excellent eating." Along the same lines, Austin adds that robins were sold in eastern U.S. markets for sixty cents a dozen as recently as 1913, but things had changed by 1961, when he wrote, "Most Americans today would as soon think of eating the family dog."

Investigating the cultural evolution that removed the robin from the dinner table and enshrined it, instead, next to our hearts is beyond the scope of this essay. But the fact remains that, today, the robin (along with another thrush, the bluebird) is one of our best-known and best-loved birds. For good reason. Everything the robin does in endearing.

It arrives early at its breeding grounds to herald the arrival of spring with its characteristic and melodious song. *Cheery, cheery* is a favorite rendering or, even better, *cheerily, cheer up, cheer up, cheerily, cheer up* — either one of which does a fine job of blending sound and sense. (The same cannot be said of the version Forbush furnishes: *kill 'em, cure 'em, give 'em physic*). In any case, the distinction of the robin's song is enhanced by the fact that it is the first bird to welcome the morning and the last to say goodbye to the parting day. Interestingly, the robin's song is at its richest from the beginning of courtship until the moment the young hatch, at which point it suddenly stops, only to resume once the fledglings leave the nest. I suspect this hiatus is due to the fact that (according to *Life Histories*) during its two weeks in the nest, each young bird consumes a total of 3.2 pounds of food. I figure that's comparable to a human baby eating an elephant, and the daddy who's bringing home that kind of bacon isn't likely to have much time for singing.

Also, the robin courts his mate with gallantry and fervor. Everybody in the countryside, says Forbush, has witnessed "the pursuit, the battles of the jealous rival males and the apparent lack of interest shown by the demure females." Audubon writes that he has often seen the robin "at the earliest dawn of a May morning, strutting around [his mate] with all the pomposity of a pigeon." To say nothing of what contemporary ornithologists call the pair's "ceremonial gaping," whereby male and female approach each other and touch their wide-open bills together.

Then, too, once they are paired, robins, like wrens, have the engaging habit of building their nests where we can all enjoy them. Instead of retreating from the advance of civilization, the robin adapted, accepting people as neighbors and people-made structures for its nest

American Robin (John James Audubon, The Birds of America, vols. 1–4, Special Collections, University Library System, University of Pittsburgh)

sites. And, again like wrens, they'll build just about anywhere. (She will build, I should say, since this is the female's job, the male's contribution consisting of bringing in nesting materials and dropping them at the site.) The point is, whether on fence post, garage shelf, or barn beam, the robin will build where we can watch and where we can steal a glimpse of eggs so pretty they've given their name to that striking blue-green color.

Even their feeding habits are entertaining. Bent vividly describes the robin on the village common in the New England summer, running quickly along with its back parallel to the ground, suddenly stopping short, then cocking its head as if to listen. Sensing a meal in the offing, "the robin thrusts his bill deep among the grass blades, prods about the roots and, seizing a worm, leans backward, and bracing his feet against the pull, carefully draws the worm from the ground." Writing in *The Birds of North America Online*, Sallabanks and James so systemize this procedure as to make it seem downright robotic: "In Head-Cocking, one eye points toward a spot on the ground 3–5 cm directly in front of the bird. . . . After holding this position for a few seconds, the robin rotates and flexes its head to bring the other eye into a similar relationship with the ground. Bill-Pouncing then occurs, whereby the bill is thrust quickly into the ground, presumably at visually detected prey, at the spot where the eyes had been directed."

Finally, there is what Audubon calls "the gentle and lively disposition of the Robin when raised in the cage." It will sing even in confinement and, once tamed, "will follow its owner, and come to his call, peck at his finger, or kiss his mouth, with seeming pleasure."

The only problem with all these charming qualities of the robin is that I, nestled deep in my woodland sanctuary, get to enjoy *none* of them. Since the American robin breeds up north and only winters here, I never hear it sing, never see its courtship, never find its beautiful eggs, and never witness its tug-of-war with earthworms. True, the southern subspecies (*Turdus migratorius achrusterus*) does breed in the Deep South, but, as Burleigh points out, this bird's discovery of the amenities of town life has rendered it utterly cosmopolitan, to the point that it's now hard to find one outside the city limits. (In fact, I hadn't seen a robin during the summer in so long that I had forgotten about the existence of the southern variety. I was reminded just recently, on an afternoon in late May during a visit with brother Richard, who clings to a tiny island of old family property in the middle of Atlanta's suburban seas. As we walked through his garden, he mentioned that he expected a fine crop of blueberries this summer if the robins didn't get them first. "You've got robins during the summer?" I asked. It wasn't a great question.)

The *American* robin, in any case, bestows all its breeding-season charms upon our neighbors to the north—which makes it ironic, I suppose, that the catastrophe that befell the robin took place largely up there. Writing in 1961, Austin lamented that despite its status as a favorite songbird, the robin's "existence is now threatened seriously by the wholesale broadcasting of new powerful insecticides, whose residual effects, long after they have stopped working on the insects, kill birds." He was talking about DDT and the other chlorinated hydrocarbons, which, as they leach into the soil, get into the systems of earthworms and poison the robins and other birds that eat the worms. Towns that fog with these chemical pesticides, says Austin, have all but wiped out their robin populations.

A year later, in *Silent Spring*, Rachel Carson told the story in all its depressing detail. It began in 1930, when so-called Dutch elm disease entered the United States from Europe on a shipment of elm burl for the veneer industry. It's a fungus disease, spread from sick trees to healthy ones by the elm bark beetle, which gets covered with the fungal spores and carries them wherever it goes. To save the trees, it seemed clear that the beetles would have to be killed, so "in community after community, especially throughout the strongholds of the American elm, the Midwest and New England, intensive spraying has become a routine procedure."

A couple of ornithologists at Michigan State first realized what the spraying was doing to the robins. The program began in 1954, and the following spring the birds migrated in as usual. But something was wrong. Dead and dying birds littered the campus, and few were seen assembling at their roosting spots. Worse, the birds weren't nesting like usual, and very few young appeared. The spraying, which was not *supposed* to be harmful to birds, continued the following spring, and the one after that, and the one after that, and the robins continued to die. In the summer of 1957, John Mehner, who had been tracking the decline, was able to locate only a single young robin—as opposed to the almost 400 young that would have populated the campus before the spraying began.

The problem was difficult to solve because the spray was not, in fact, killing the robins. Here's what was happening, according to Carson's account: The spray covered the elm leaves in a sticky film impervious to rain. When the leaves fell and decomposed, earthworms fed in the leaf litter, accumulating the DDT in their bodies in such high concentrations that a mere eleven worms could provide a lethal dose of poison to a foraging robin. In addition to those killed outright, untold numbers of birds were rendered sterile by the poison. This scenario was being played out wherever DDT was being used to wipe out the elm bark beetle.

Carson's book helped spark the public protest that led to the U.S. ban of DDT in 1972, but the harm done in the meantime is hard to calculate. Recent research indicates that it probably took from ten to seventeen years for robin populations to return to pre-DDT levels in areas where spraying took place, and that DDT stays in the soil so long that earthworms may still be passing it to robins thirty years after a single application.

The good news is that the robin is a hardy, adaptable species and that, across the continent, its population is widely distributed, healthy, and stable. The bad news—witness the killing of 10,000 robins by Azodrin, one of the organophospates, in a field near Homestead, Florida, in the 1970s—is that there is no end to the folly of the human species.

Carolina Chickadee
Parus carolinensis

Tufted Titmouse
Parus bicolor

Unversed in the arcane science of morphology, I have no idea why the chickadee and the titmouse are both members of the *Parus* family. Here's what I do know: "Titmouse" comes from Anglo-Saxon; the first part, "tit," refers generally to anything small, and "mouse" is a corruption of "mase," the name given to any number of small birds. Put them together and you have, well, "small small bird."

Perhaps by the time Linnaeus came along, the Brits were already referring to both chickadees and titmice (both being small birds) as "titmice" or, more properly, "titmouses." In any event, he named the family *Parus* (which means "a titmouse"), and the family includes both species. Under discussion here are the Carolina chickadee (*Parus carolinensis*, or "titmouse of Carolina") and the tufted titmouse (*Parus bicolor*, or "titmouse of two colors," which, since the bird has at least four colors that leap readily to the eye, makes as little sense as all the rest).

Now, as for the birds themselves.

Back during the early summer, I spent the better part of a day trying to find the nest of a pair of Carolina chickadees. I had watched them zipping back and forth from the feeders at the south end of the house to the edge of the woods on the north side, so I had a pretty good idea where to look. I stepped into the trees with my binoculars and finally saw one (or thought I saw one) disappear into a knot-hole of a maple tree, maybe twenty-five feet off the ground. They're cavity-nesters, so that made sense, but it wasn't very satisfying. These birds typically nest just a few feet off the ground where you can see something. But not this pair. No. Not in my backyard. This was fairly typical of my nest-discovery efforts.

About that time Nina Morgan called to say that she and her hus-

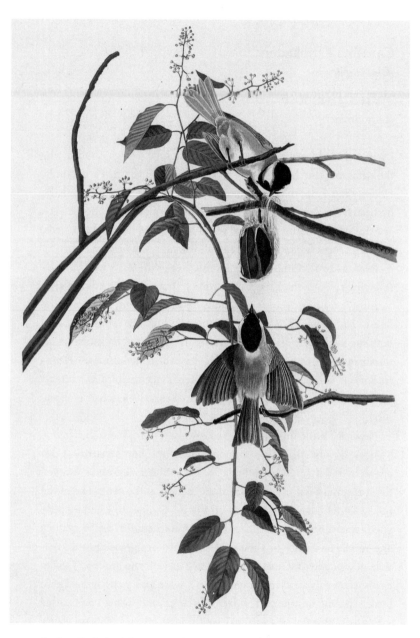

Carolina Chickadee (John James Audubon, The Birds of America, vols. 1–4, Special Collections, University Library System, University of Pittsburgh)

band, Peter, were at that moment watching a couple of chickadees build a nest. "Where?" I asked. Well, it seems that they had this old birdhouse that they hadn't gotten around to putting up and had just left lying on their front stoop. Now the chickadees were moving in. *Sheeesh.* I've got two charming birdhouses, carefully situated in the most inviting locales, that no bird has ever deigned to enter. A few weeks later Peter rubbed my nose in it by e-mailing me digital pictures of the fledglings—little balls of fluffy feathers, their black caps slightly unsettled—posing on the brick steps.

The Carolina chickadee is the one we have here in the South, I am told, and the black-capped chickadee is the more northern variety. There ain't a lot of difference between them. The black-capped may be a centimeter longer, and, if the light is right, you might be able to discern a little white in its wing; but, honestly, if both birds were on my feeder at the same time, I doubt if I could tell them apart.

In fact, for a while I was pretty sure I had a black-cap in my woods. I thought I had heard or read somewhere that while both species utter the familiar *chickadee-dee-dee* call, only the black-cap is capable of the beautiful, high-pitched, two-note whistle often represented as *fee-bee*, with the first note higher than the second. But I was sure I had heard that whistle, and even surer when I actually saw a chickadee perched on a limb whistling it. (This is not an easy thing to see, since chickadees don't stay still very long.) Turns out I was misinformed. The experts tell me that the two species whistle almost identically, but not quite. As bird musicologist Aretas Saunders explains in *Life Histories*, "The Carolina chickadee's song consists of two clear whistled notes, but each one is either introduced or followed by a shorter, lower-pitched sibilant note. That is, instead of the bird singing a simple *fee-bee*, it sings *sufee-subee* or else *feesu beesu*." Some observers, he adds, have failed to notice these quiet sibilants and have concluded that there is "no essential difference in the song of this chickadee and the blackcap." Feel free to count me among the hearing-impaired.

Whichever, everybody loves the busy little chickadee. Its lively chatter keeps us company summer and winter—which perhaps explains why this bird is a special favorite of nature-themed Christmas cards. It appreciates the feeder during the cold months, but at other seasons, when it has a choice, it's a regular insect gourmand, devouring plant lice, scale, weevils, ants, wasps, spiders, and grasshoppers by the zillions. "No bug is too small to escape its penetrating eyes," as Forbush puts it. And in the springtime, foraging acrobatically for the silky casings on the undersides of the freshly sprouted leaves, these birds might consume a thousand insect eggs in a single day.

I've read that they even love tent caterpillars, but based on my own observations, I'm not sure "love" is the right word. I had two "tents" in my cherry tree last spring, and in the middle of April I watched in horror as the black, hairy caterpillars began to emerge. *Where are the cuckoos?* I hollered in despair. The voracious, defoliating beasts were marching out the clean limbs of the cherry tree like some implacable army, single file, unrelenting, an endless horde. It was actually too early for the cuckoos, as I realized, but surely some other caterpillar-loving bird would step into the breach. The tree was absolutely full of goldfinches. The goldfinches got out of the way. A vireo seemed momentarily interested in one of the tents, poked about a bit, but returned empty-billed to the treetops. Then, finally, *yes!*—I saw a chickadee with one of the caterpillars dangling from its beak like a long handlebar mustache. But did he *love* it? Frankly, he seemed not quite sure what to do with it, and neither he nor any of his kin came back for more. *Tolerated* it, maybe.

Both the Carolina and the black-capped are cavity-nesters, as noted. Early in the spring they begin their search for some soft wood (where a limb has decayed and fallen, for example, or maybe even a weak spot in an old fence post) that they can dig away at with their little beaks. Both male and female work hard at the job, and the result is a hole as much as ten inches deep. According to *Life Histories*, "The little bird is wise enough to carry the telltale chips away and scatter them far and wide—something the woodpeckers are less careful about." Once the cavity is ready, the female finishes the job by cozily lining her nest with plant fibers, moss, feathers, insect cocoons, and maybe, if she can find it, a bit of rabbit fur. The completed nest sports a curious architectural amenity: One side of the lining is built up higher than the other, which furnishes a flap that can be folded over to cover the eggs when the parent is away. The flap serves to fool predators into thinking the nest is empty, and, later, it gives the nest a flat floor suitable for roosting.

Green calls the chickadee a "secretive nester" that prefers deeper woods than the titmouse or wren, which may explain my trouble locating their nest. But other writers have observed that, increasingly, this bird is making use of man-made structures like clothesline pipes or prefab birdhouses, which no doubt explains the Morgans' undeserved good fortune.

The Morgans aren't alone in having watched chickadee nest-building, though; these birds don't seem to mind people in the least. "The embodiment of cheerfulness, verve and courage," writes Forbush, and they're so inquisitive that by imitating the *fee-bee* whistle, or by "making a sucking sound on the back of your hand," you'll soon have them flitting and chattering on the limbs right over your head. This trick sounds like what brother Richard calls "pishing": Stand still in your selected birding spot, make a simple *psh-psh-psh-psh* sound for a few seconds, and not only chickadees but a number of other species, too, will come to investigate. He believes that it's a defensive behavior; the birds associate the noise with danger, and once they've come to see what the danger is, they can safely fly away from it.

I suspect Richard is right, but the chickadee by all accounts is an unusually plucky little bird. In his passage about the woodchopper with whom he struck up a friendship, Thoreau writes that as the man sat on a log to eat his dinner, "the chickadees would sometimes come round and alight on his arm and peck at the potato in his fingers." John Woodcock reported in *Life Histories* that he induced a chickadee to take a piece of nut from between his fingertips, and "two days later he would perch on my finger and take a nut from between my teeth, or would sit on a branch and let me touch him while he was eating a nut." Eventually, this guy had a dozen chickadees following him around, which, he says, made for an interesting scene when he brought out his .22 to hunt rabbits. Gathering around him, "they made aiming almost impossible, for every time I raised the rifle, one or two birds would perch on the barrel completely hiding the sights."

Too cute for its own good? Daring to the point of foolhardiness? Maybe. But the chickadee has also got some street smarts. It is on record as being one of the few birds that can find its way back out of the "Government-type" sparrow trap, which has an entrance of inward-sloping wires on the bottom. In experiments reported in *Life Histories*, the chickadee was quick to find the entrance, dart in and grab a sunflower seed, and "with little investigation" dart back out again to find a convenient perch to crack and eat its seed. "They rarely became confused as did the juncos, tree sparrows, and purple finches." Along the same lines, if a chickadee finds itself inside our screened porch in its search for insects, it'll find its way right back out again—unlike the easily panicked wrens and phoebes.

Maybe that's why so many other winter birds—the titmice, the nuthatches, the downy woodpeckers, and even the sweet-trilling pine warblers—like to hang around with the chickadee gang. Maybe they're awestruck. They haven't got the nerve to spit in the devil's eye, but they like to watch.

LET ME AMEND THAT. Whatever motives those other birds might have for hanging around with chickadees, the tufted titmouse would be the last bird in the world to stand in awe of its little cousin. Because whatever the chickadee does, the titmouse does it more, bigger, better, or louder.

Start with whistling. Lower pitched (and somehow less enchanting) than the chickadee's *fee-bee*, the titmouse's *peter-peter-peter* is equally clear and distinctive, but louder and much more frequently heard. (The titmice in my woods, by the way, put very little emphasis on the second syllable, so that I would be inclined to render it *peet, peet, peet*.) Bent says it sounds like a man whistling up his dog, an apt comparison, but adds that during mating season in early spring the sound is so constant as to become monotonous and tiresome. I don't know about that. Like the chickadee, the titmouse is a restless little

Tufted Titmouse (John James Audubon, The Birds of America, *vols. 1–4, Special Collections, University Library System, University of Pittsburgh)*

bird, and it wasn't easy for me to put bird and whistle together. When I finally identified the source of the whistle I had become familiar with, I was gratified, and I don't think I could ever find the sound annoying. (It's easy to imitate if you're a decent whistler, and the titmouse will set up a nice duet with you.)

In the titmouse's feeding habits, we have another case of "more is more." Like its cousin, the titmouse prefers insects when it can get them, but summer or winter you'll see it at the feeder more often than the chickadee. Why? Because it's not only eating, it's storing. According to *The Birds of North America Online*, titmice shell those sunflower seeds and then hide the kernels in tree trunks and limbs all over their territory. (Neither chickadees nor titmice can sit on the feeder and munch away like the grosbeaks can, by the way. Both have to take up a single seed and carry it to a nearby branch, where they hold it in place with their feet and peck away at it until they break it open. In fact, both species spend a lot of time at this activity, in case you're inclined to watch.)

According to my own observations, the titmouse outdoes the chickadee in insect-eating, too. As I mentioned, I was amused to watch a chickadee take on a tent caterpillar, but damned if I didn't see a titmouse go after a tiger swallowtail. It was a little earlier in the year, late March, and the cherry tree in bloom, with all manner of bees and butterflies wallowing in the nectar. I watched the titmouse launch out, pick the big swallowtail out of the air, carry it back to a limb, and eat it right up. The pretty yellow wings fluttered away in the breeze as the bird concentrated on the meat. Looking again a couple of hours later, I saw another tiger swallowtail working the cherry blossoms, settling itself, spreading its wings wide, presenting an inviting target. Sure enough: *Zap*—the titmouse struck again. But somehow it missed this time, and the butterfly fluttered away to safety. Maybe they're not as easy to catch as you'd think, and maybe that's why, though both the cherry tree and the azaleas below it were full of both swallowtails and titmice, I never saw the bird take another butterfly.

Evidence suggests that the titmouse is smarter than its cousin as well. It's the chickadee's equal when it has to find its way back out of banding traps, and it has been shown to have a remarkable problem-solving ability when food is the reward. What's more, Green writes that one member of the family, the varied titmouse, is the little bird the Japanese train to tell fortunes at their shrine festivals and street fairs. "At the command of its master it hops to its perch, takes a coin from your fingers, drops it into a cash box, opens the door of a minia-ture shrine, takes out your paper fortune, and tears off the wrapping so you receive it ready to read."

The two species have a lot in common when it comes to nest-building. The titmouse, like the chickadee, is a cavity-nester, but the titmouse usually nests higher and is more inclined to use a hole pre-viously occupied by a woodpecker or even a squirrel. To some extent the two species use similar nesting materials—leaves, fibers, mosses, dry grass—but the titmouse is never entirely satisfied with plant ma-terial and ranges wide for more exotic matter, such as wool, cotton, fur, hair, and often snakeskin. If the source of these prized materi-als happens to be living fauna, so much the better. One early April evening I was sitting very quietly on the front porch, listening to the *picky-tucky-tuck* of the summer tanager, wondering if she would build again in the pear tree. Moses, our long-haired golden-mix, exhausted from a long day of whining for attention, lay asleep at my feet. Sud-denly a titmouse lit on the edge of the porch, took two or three quick hops closer, and plucked a few hairs from the dog's luxuriant tail. Moses jerked awake, but the bird was long gone.

Apparently such brazen behavior is typical. Less typical, presum-ably, is the experience of E. Irwin Smith, a contributor to *Life Histo-ries*. Smith writes that he was sitting on a stump at the edge of the woods when a titmouse began flitting around his head. After two reconnoitering missions, "it lit on my head, and, in a very diligent manner, began to pick the hairs therefrom. The pricking of its sharp little toes on my scalp and the vigor of the hair-pulling was a trifle too much for my self-control, and I instinctively moved my head. Away it flew, but only for a moment, and then it was back at work, harder than before."

As this anecdote suggests, while the chickadee gets close, the titmouse gets closer. Practically everybody knows somebody who has had a titmouse take food right out of his or her hand. Thoreau wrote of the chickadee that ate the potato off the woodchopper's fingers; he also wrote of the titmice that would pick insects off his firewood even as he was carrying it inside to throw it on the fire. One of Bent's correspondents describes the titmouse as "the friendliest of all our southern birds, exceeding the Carolina chickadee by far." Okay. But define "friendly." Watching the titmouse on the feeder, where it tends to stand its ground against all comers, "aggressive" might be the word that comes to mind. But nobody wants to apply a pejorative to the curious, comical little bird with the bright black eyes. Nobody, that is, except Audubon. "The Crested Titmouse," he writes, "is of a rather vicious disposition, which sometimes prompts it to attack smaller birds, and destroy them by thumping their heads with its bill until it breaks the skull."

Gee, J. J., I don't know. Maybe those smaller birds made the mistake of coming too close to the titmouse's nest, which the female defends so staunchly that it's virtually impossible to flush her. Or maybe they threatened the titmouse children, which the parents not only raise protectively but hold close in the family bosom all through the summer and fall.

No, I don't think I'm buying "vicious," just as "friendly" seems to go too far in the other direction. But bold? Assertive? Inquisitive? Intelligent? Yes, yes, yes, yes. And a damn fine whistler to boot. In other words, the chickadee times two.

So maybe it makes sense, after all, that the family name, *Parus*, means "titmouse." And we'll leave it to the morphologists to explain why the chickadee belongs.

Osprey
*Pandion haliaetus**

Here we see the advantage of armchair birding. Like any inlander who has taken a vacation on the Atlantic coast, I've seen the osprey. Nearing the shore, I've seen its imposing nests somehow resting on top of telephone and electric poles. I've even had the privilege of seeing it rise from the water with a fish in its talons. Still, if I had to rely solely on my own observations, I would have much left to learn about this beautiful, talented, industrious, and oddly civilized predator.

Remarkable in many ways, the osprey, or "fish hawk," as Audubon calls it, stands alone as the only North American raptor that earns virtually all of its living by catching live fish. And it does it the hard way—not like the great blue heron, which stands motionless in shallow water and waits for the fish to come to it, nor like the brown pelican, which does take the trouble to dive, but catches the fish in its bill and then has the luxury of settling comfortably on the waves. The masterful osprey folds its wings and plummets like a meteor, often from higher than a hundred feet; hits the water feetfirst; and, more often than not, succeeds in sinking its talons into its unsuspecting prey. Sometimes its dive takes it all the way under; in any case, grasping its fish always head-forward—to reduce wind resistance?—it must rise again, shaking the heavy water from its feathers, and carry its catch to nest or feeding roost.

Easier pickings are no doubt available, but this is a bird of refined palate. As Austin puts it, the osprey will deign to pick up a dead fish only if it is still fresh. "Unlike the Bald Eagle, it will not touch a fish that has started to go bad." (Conversely, just about the only live fish the bald eagle eats are those it steals from the osprey.) Audubon cites an interesting example of the osprey's willingness to eat dead

---

*Ernest Choate, in *The Dictionary of American Bird Names*, tells the funny, but lengthy, story of the misguided creation of the genus *Pandion* by French ornithologist Savigny. If you're interested, I highly recommend the book. If you're *that* interested, you probably already have it.

but "still fresh" fish. On their southward migration, he writes, the ospreys pause over the Mississippi lakes where the wood ibis are wintering. These birds "wade among the water in immense flocks, and so trample the bottom as to convert the lakes into filthy puddles, in which the fishes are unable to respire with ease." The dying fish rise to the surface in such numbers that "not only are the Ibises plentifully supplied, but Vultures, Eagles, and Fish Hawks, come to participate in the spoil."

Come late winter, the osprey returns to its breeding grounds, where, in all likelihood, it will find its previous year's nest waiting. It's a huge thing, with a foundation more of limbs than sticks (some of them four feet long, says Bent, and thick as a man's wrist) and the interior padded with seaweed, sod, and just about anything else the bird can pick up. In *Eastern Birds' Nests*, Harrison lists some of the odd items found in osprey nests — "rope, broom, barrel staves, hoops, fishnet, toy boat, old shoes, straw hat, rag doll, bottles, tin cans, shells, sponges, etc" — and recalls John Steinbeck's report that he discovered three shirts, one bath towel, one arrow, and his rake in an osprey nest in his garden.

Though the osprey pair like to reuse the same nest year after year, these industrious birds are certainly not going to move back in without sprucing the place up a bit. The female sends her mate out to bring in a few new things (a bed frame, maybe? a clock radio?), and she arranges them to suit her taste. As a result, the osprey's nest, already sizable, grows a little bigger every year, and the years continue to roll by. More than one writer has reported the existence of osprey nests forty years old and, thanks to the annual increment, as much as ten feet high. These monstrous edifices eventually collapse of their own weight and crash to the ground, sometimes bringing the tree down with them. (Could the same pair of birds have used the same nest for forty years? Possibly, says Austin, given that the osprey at one time held the age record for a banded bird at twenty-one years.)

Osprey (John James Audubon, The Birds of America, vols. 1–4, Special Collections, University Library System, University of Pittsburgh)

In fact, the osprey's nest is so large as to have apartments available for rent. You might well find the nests of starlings or grackles or other opportunistic species tucked into the outer wall. Audubon attributes this odd circumstance to the osprey's surprisingly mild disposition. "I have never observed a Fish Hawk chasing any other bird whatever," he writes. Likewise, Bent says the subletting is possible only because the osprey is such a "peaceful, gentle, and harmless neighbor." What's odd to me, though, is that the tenants have somehow intuited their landlord's good nature and feel safe in such an environment. After all, the osprey, roughly the size of the red-tailed hawk, is equipped with the same hooked beak and razor-sharp talons of the many predators that make smaller birds a mainstay of their diet.

But perhaps that's not to be wondered at. Except where its food and family are concerned, the osprey apparently espouses the great dictum of civilized society: Live and let live. Its kindness is repaid by a universe in which it has virtually no enemies—except for the occasional member of the human species who collects its beautiful eggs. As long as fishing grounds are within convenient reach, the osprey is happy to nest on farms or in other human habitats, where it might build on old chimneys, windmill towers, sheds, barns, fences, walls, piles of debris, or just about anywhere. The farmer, in turn, cultivates the relationship because, at least during its nesting season, the osprey will drive any chicken-minded hawk from the vicinity. More than that, says Bent, the farm-dwelling osprey will sometimes make a fine "watch-bird." It seems to recognize and accept with equanimity the farm's human residents but raises a ruckus at the approach of strangers.

Given this bird's other refinements, it comes as no surprise that the osprey is a model of fidelity—monogamous, mated for life, and reluctant to take another spouse even in the event of tragedy. Bent tells the story of one male, who, having lost his brooding mate to a lightning strike, took up a station on top of a nearby tree and kept his lonely vigil there all summer long. In September he joined the seasonal migration, but the next spring he returned to his treetop post, where he again stayed the entire season, presumably still mourning his loss.

Barring such disaster, the female will lay her three pretty eggs and incubate them for some four weeks, while her mate hunts and fetches. Like any good husband heading off to the office, he likes to leave his wife with a display of his affection. He rises high in the sky, writes Audubon, "utters a loud shriek," and dives downward again. Right before reaching the nest, he spreads his wings and tail and "glides towards his beloved female, in a beautifully curved line. The female partially raises herself from her eggs, emits a low cry, resumes her former posture, and her delighted partner flies off to the sea, to seek a favourite fish for her whom he loves."

Understandably, the children are disinclined to leave such a happy home, and the parents are in no hurry to push them out the door. In fact, Bent believes that during their two months in the nest they not only ingest the food their parents provide but also absorb their parents' impeccable manners. "Their good nature comes early," he observes. At a few weeks old, when they begin to feed themselves (that is, when the parent drops a fish in the nest and flies away, instead of tearing it up for them), they "seem to take turns," showing a restraint surprising among adolescents of any species. (Much as I love that picture of avian gentility — "After you." "No, you go ahead, please." — contemporary research indicates that such civilized behavior lasts only as long as food is plentiful. In leaner times, older nestlings are quick to dominate younger by pecking them into submission, then gobbling up all the food they can hold even if it means starvation for their smaller siblings.)

Eventually, of course, the young must make their own way in the world — all the more difficult since these pampered fledglings have never followed their parents on a fishing expedition to see how it's done. The lack of instruction is sometimes comically evident, says Forbush, who watched a young osprey dive and miss seven times in a row. Nevertheless, perhaps a further measure of the osprey's sanguine outlook, "the bird did not appear to be in the least discouraged." In any case, the young will have all of late summer and early fall to master their craft, at which point they'll be ready to join their elders for the long migration to the fish-rich waters of Central and South America. The following season, they'll return to nesting grounds spanning the continent from Maine to Alaska and down the coastlines all the way to Baja, Mexico, in the West and the tip of Florida in the East.

And that's just its North American range. In fact, the osprey is found on every continent except Antarctica, and its wide distribution no doubt helped sustain it during "the pestilence"—that is, the DDT days of the 1960s and 1970s. Eggshell thinning caused by the poison decimated osprey populations along the New York–Massachusetts coastline, in the Chesapeake Bay, and in the Great Lakes, among other areas. On the other hand, the spectacular devastation helped galvanize opposition to the use of this noxious pesticide. After DDT was banned in 1972, the bird's North American population recovered rapidly.

So those of you who live along a lake or shoreline might yet be treated to an odd and marvelous sight. Watch for the beautiful bird, circling over the water, to fold its wings and glide toward the surface in a long, gentle sweep. Watch it drop its legs just enough for its feet to drag through the water—for maybe twenty yards or so. What is it doing? Well, it has eaten. Now it must wash. Such is the nature of the osprey.

Red-Tailed Hawk
Buteo jamaicensis

Cooper's Hawk
Accipiter cooperii

But which hawk is the chicken hawk? Is it the buteo (buzzard hawk), typified by the red-tailed hawk and its smaller cousin the red-shouldered hawk, or is it the accipiter (bird hawk), typified by the Cooper's hawk and its smaller cousin the sharp-shinned hawk?

Audubon gave his vote to the red-tailed hawk. Once the kingbird has raised its brood and is no longer on high alert, he writes, the redtail "visits the farm-houses, to pay his regards to the poultry." He swoops down indiscriminately upon the young chickens, ducklings, and turkeys, or, when they are not available, he'll go after the older fowl, "the dying screams of which are heard by the farmer at the plough, who swears vengeance against the robber."

Audubon then offers a set piece in which the farmer, recalling the location of the hawk's nest, goes after the bird with rifle and axe. Apparently aggravated beyond all reason, he sets about felling the mighty oak tree. When the frightened female shows herself at the edge of the nest, he guns her down, then finishes off the tree to make sure the young don't survive. With the "noble tree" crashing to the ground with such force as to shake the earth, "the work of revenge is now accomplished: the farmer seizes the younglings, and carries them home, to be tormented by his children, until death terminates their brief career."

Not without reason, according to Audubon, do American farmers call the redtail the "hen-hawk." For good measure, he adds that Louisiana creoles call it the *grand mangeur de poules* (that is, "big eater of chickens").

A century later, though, attitudes toward the big buteo had changed—at least among the experts. Bent wrote that it was now "generally conceded that the red-tailed hawk is a highly beneficial

species, as its food consists mainly of injurious rodents and as it does very little damage to domestic poultry or wild birds." Professor Beal's examinations confirmed that rodents and other small mammals provided 85 percent of the redtail's diet. Bent and other writers were more worried about what the farmer's prejudice was doing to the redtail's population than about what the redtail was doing to the chicken population.

The redtail, after all, is a bird so skittish that you can't get within a hundred yards of one. Audubon believed that it was particularly wary of anybody carrying a gun, "the use of which it seems to understand perfectly," and that at the approach of such an intruder, "it spreads its wings, utters a loud shriek, and sails off in an opposite direction." I don't seem to need a gun, though, to keep the pair in my woods at bay. I see them regularly from my window, scudding over the treetops or circling above, but they're nowhere around when I'm out walking the property. Once or twice I've earned a scolding; I've heard the bird's impressive long-drawn *kee-aarrr-r-r-r* and seen one looking down on me from a treetop high above. But if that means I've come too close to its nest, it would be news to me. I've looked hard during late winter and early spring, when the trees are still bare and these early nesters are supposed to be at it. I've even looked, as Bent advises, for the telltale circle of white on the ground below, but I've looked in vain.

Even if I could find it, I'd be unlikely to observe any nesting activity. The birds would be long gone at the first sign of my approach. Bent says that if you want to study the home life of these birds, you need a blind that offers "absolute concealment." In fact, even after the young have hatched, the adults are quick to fly and hesitant to return once they've been disturbed. Bent accuses them of being "much more concerned about their own safety than about the welfare of their eggs or young"; then, to redeem them, he mentions this curious habit: Every day, while the chicks are young, the parents bring a fresh

Red-Tailed Hawk (John James Audubon, The Birds of America, vols. 1–4, Special Collections, University Library System, University of Pittsburgh)

green bough to the nest, apparently either to shade the young from the sun or to conceal them from predators.

I don't get to see any of that. But that's okay. It's enough to know that these regal birds are living in my old oak and beech trees. I don't figure ever to see the adult pair hunt together, either, which Audubon assures me that they like to do. Apparently, the squirrel that hopes to escape by scrambling to the far side of the tree trunk is doomed. If the one don't get him, the other'n will. "Unless it immediately finds a hole into which to retreat, it is caught in a few minutes, killed, carried to the nest, torn in pieces, and distributed among the young Hawks." I'm happy to imagine it. Lord knows I've got more than enough of squirrels.

What all this adds up to, for me, is that the red-tailed hawk is a cautious, prudent bird, content to hunt the deep woods and keep people and people's doings at a distance. It is also a spectacularly beautiful bird and, if I may say so, probably the repository of the soul of my dear deceased friend Ben Tucker. (I base that supposition on the fact that I think of Ben every time I see a redtail soaring overhead in a sunlit sky, its broad rust-red tail spread in glory.) In any case, Ben Tucker was no chicken-thieving lowlife, and I hereby conclude and declare, with apologies to Audubon, that the red-tailed hawk isn't either.

That leaves the Cooper.

I HADN'T BEEN OUT YET to refill the suet feeder on this chilly February morning, so a downy woodpecker took up a position in the cherry tree next to the seed feeder, maybe wondering if a sunflower kernel might do in a pinch. It might have noticed that the red-bellied woodpeckers like the seeds just fine. But before it could make up its mind, there was a sudden commotion—a quick explosion of motion—and the little woodpecker was gone.

No. He wasn't gone. He was on the ground, pinned there by a

Cooper's Hawk (John James Audubon, The Birds of America, *vols. 1–4, Special Collections, University Library System, University of Pittsburgh)*

Cooper's hawk. To be precise, the hawk had the downy on its back and appeared to be treading on its wings as if to spread it open and completely expose its underside. Here the scientist in me quailed. I banged on my window frame, thinking to scare the hawk away and save the downy. Of course, the hawk flew away *with* the downy. I really should've watched, I suppose, but Audubon, describing a peregrine falcon in similar circumstances, gives me a pretty good idea of what I missed: "No sooner is the prey dead than the Falcon turns its belly upward, and begins to pluck it with his bill, which he does very expertly, holding it meantime quite fast in his talons; and as soon as a portion is cleared of feathers, tears the flesh in large pieces, and swallows it with great avidity." If I had read Audubon earlier — "Should he be approached by an enemy, he rises with [his prey] and flies off into the interior of the woods" — I would have known I had no chance to save the downy.

When I told this story to Don Hastings, Atlanta's noted horticulturist, he was quick to one-up me. A Cooper's hawk swooped down on his feeder, he said, and delivered a deathblow to a chickadee. The little bird slipped from the Cooper's grasp as he rose with it, but he caught it again before it hit the ground. E. B. White, in his essay "Mr. Forbush's Friends," two-upped me. He cited an instance in which a Cooper's hawk plunged a flicker into a roadside ditch containing one foot of water and held it under for three minutes. (*The Birds of North America Online*, incidentally, confirms this incredible killing technique.) Nestlings, presumably, are no less at risk. *Life Histories* reports that a Cooper's hawk raided a mockingbird's nest four times over a period of three days and "absconded with all four babies one after the other, despite all the scolding the parents were capable of."

The only question left unanswered there is what else the hawk ate during those three days. For this rapacious marauder, one and a third baby birds a day ain't likely to cut it. Bent tells of one raised in captivity that, when it was six weeks old, ate nine English sparrows and a common mouse in one day. Over the next four weeks, it averaged eight sparrows a day. "It particularly savored the entrails," says Bent, "tearing the bird apart in order to get at them first." If the food was still warm and the blood uncoagulated, "it tore it open and apparently bathed the bill in the blood and the visceral juices. It apparently sucked up these fluids in order to allay thirst," all the while refusing to drink water. (Is this the place to mention that the female Cooper is one-third larger than the male, and, presumably, one-third more bloodthirsty?)

Okay. The Cooper's hawk loves gore, but does it love chickens? Since I have no chickens, I'll have to defer to the opinions of the experts. (I'd love to have some chickens, by the way, and all the more so because they would gobble up the Japanese beetles that defoliate my little apple tree every summer, but Peanut, as I believe I have mentioned elsewhere, is a chicken killer, and that's that.)

Bent, for one, declares that the Cooper is indeed the "essential chicken hawk, so cordially hated by poultry farmers, and is the principal cause of the widespread antipathy toward hawks in general." This hawk, he says, does more damage to poultry than all other hawks put together and also has a special fondness for domestic pigeons and young ducks. Forbush agrees that the Cooper's hawk takes more poultry than any other hawk, but it often manages to avoid blame. "The thievery of the Cooper's Hawk is so adroit that often the bird is not seen or suspected, while the soaring hawks, such as the Red-shouldered or the Red-tailed, have to pay the penalty, because they are so conspicuous and may be seen occasionally soaring over the hen-yard." Green, too, notes that it's the Cooper that gives hawks in general a bad name. "Known also as blue darter, blue-tailed hawk, and chicken hawk, the Cooper's hawk is hated by man and bird under all three names."

Et cetera. So the question has been decided. The Cooper's hawk is the bane of the chicken yard. But is that all that's to be said? Isn't it a remarkable, even awesome, bird for all that? Don't you have to admire a bird that brings such verve and single-mindedness to its villainy? Bent says it knows how to keep objects like trees, barns, or fencerows between itself and its prey until the last second, when it swoops in remorselessly for the kill. "It will follow a bird into a thicket," writes

Forbush, "often plunging through by sheer velocity, and so driving its victim out into the open and capturing it by its superior powers of flight, or by so terrorizing it that it becomes almost helpless from fright." My, my. You'd almost think that Thomas Harris studied the behavior of the Cooper before he created Hannibal Lecter.

Not surprisingly, the Cooper's population had declined significantly by the mid-1900s, when pesticide contamination added its toll to what people with guns had already accomplished. These days, the bird's habitat continues to diminish as forests give way to neighborhoods. Thanks to the eventual ban on DDT and its ilk (and maybe also to declining numbers of irate chicken farmers), some local populations have stabilized, but, according to *The Birds of North America Online*, the Cooper remains on "threatened" or "endangered" lists in several eastern states.

It occurs to me that it's probably harder to get up an effective pity party on behalf a bird like the Cooper than on behalf of, say, the red-cockaded woodpecker, the little bird whose plight has brought titanic timber corporations to their knees. But, hey, not every bird can keep itself alive by picking insects out of pine bark. Some have to kill spectacularly. And much as I love my little downies and chickadees and all the rest, next time the Cooper's hawk comes a-preying, I plan to watch.

The end? Already? How about all the other familiar birds, favorites like the towhee, the red-winged blackbird, the pretty little indigo bunting? How about the brown thrasher, for goodness sake, my own state's bird!

You probably think I'm trying to incite enthusiasm for a follow-up volume. How absurd. I would never be so shameless. The case is just the opposite. If I've done nothing else in these pages, I've thrown open the gates to armchair birddom, where all can enter — even without expensive binoculars.

Honestly, the end has come as planned. The eight-month sabbatical I granted myself is now over; the money set aside for the project, gone. I must say, though, I didn't foresee how perfectly the weather would conspire. A cold spell here in late February brought freezing rain two nights ago and knocked out our power — just about the time I'd sent the chicken hawks off to roost.

This morning the power's back on, but ice droplets still hang from the hoods over the dish feeders. Not that the birds care. Juncos and goldfinches cover the ground. I've got titmice and chickadees, Mr. Cardinal, a pair of downy woodpeckers, a pine warbler, and nuthatches on the suet.

It is cold, though. I go out and thump the ice off the feeders and let a couple of splinters melt in my hand. I stir the sunflower seed in the dish to make sure it's not all frozen together and scatter a little more on the ground. I break the ice sheet on the birdbath, pour it off, and refill it with water. The temperature is in the mid-30s, and the water won't refreeze until tonight.

The birds surround me, quiet in the near limbs, waiting. They're not going anywhere. Suddenly, from the upturned root-ball by the edge of the yard, I hear the Carolina wren singing at the top of its lungs: *jibberty, jibberty, jibberty, jibberty!*

The end.

The beginning.

SOURCES

Audubon, John James. *Ornithological Biography, or an Account of the Habits of the Birds of the United States of America*. Philadelphia: E. I. Carey and A. Hart, 1832. The Emory University Library in Atlanta has this wonderful book (five volumes) available on microfiche. It's possible to find a copy for sale through used or rare book vendors—if price is no object.

————. *Writings and Drawings*, selected by Christoph Irmscher. New York: Library of America, 1999.

Austin, Oliver L., Jr. *Birds of the World*. New York: Golden Press, 1961.

Barks, Coleman. *Gourd Seed*. Athens, Ga.: Maypop Books, 1993.

Bent, Arthur Cleveland. *Life Histories of North American Birds*. New York: Dover, 1962–65. The first of Bent's volumes, *Life Histories of North American Diving Birds*, appeared in 1919, and the series continued for forty years, producing twenty-one volumes in all. The work was undertaken by the Smithsonian Institution, and the volumes appeared as *Bulletins* of the United States National Museum. Dover set about reprinting all the volumes in the series in the early 1960s.

The Birds of North America Online. The print version of this comprehensive resource (eighteen volumes covering 716 species and consisting of individual accounts by many of North America's leading ornithologists) was edited by Drs. Alan Poole and Frank Gill and appeared in 2002. Published by The Birds of North America, Inc., in Philadelphia, it represents the culmination of a ten-year effort on the part of the American Ornithologists' Union, the Cornell Lab of Ornithology, and the Academy of Natural Sciences. Now, happily, thanks to the Cornell Lab, the whole thing, with audio, video, and recurrent updating, is available online—for a small annual subscription fee.

Bottoms, David. *Under the Vulture Tree*. New York: Morrow, 1987.

Burleigh, Thomas D. *Georgia Birds*. Norman: University of Oklahoma Press, 1958. This big, beautiful book is a must for southern birders, particularly with its handsome illustrations by George Miksch Sutton.

Carson, Rachel. *Silent Spring*. Boston: Houghton Mifflin, 1962.

Cashwell, Peter. *The Verb "To Bird": Sightings of an Avid Birder*. Philadelphia: Paul Dry Books, 2003.

Choate, Ernest A. *The Dictionary of American Bird Names*. Rev. ed. Boston: Harvard Common Press, 1985.

Flegg, Jim. *Birdlife: Insights into the Daily Lives of Birds*. London: Pelham Books, 1986.

Forbush, Edward Howe, and John Bichard May. *A Natural History of American Birds of Eastern and Central North America*. New York: Bramhall House, 1939. This is the abridgment of Forbush's three-volume work, with material on 100 additional species supplied by J. B. May. It retains the illustrations of Louis Agassiz Fuertes and Allan Brooks, with four new plates by Roger Tory Peterson.

Green, Charlotte Hilton. *Birds of the South: Permanent and Winter Birds*. Chapel Hill: University of North Carolina Press, 1933; reprinted 1995. Green (1889–1992) was a North Carolina naturalist whose column "Out-of-Doors in Carolina" appeared in the *Raleigh News and Observer* from 1932 to 1974. This book is a collection of some of her early writings.

Harrison, Hal H. *Eastern Birds' Nests*. Norwalk, Conn.: Easton Press, 1984. This is the special, leather-bound edition published as part of the fiftieth anniversary of the Peterson Field Guides series. The book was originally published by Houghton Mifflin in 1975.

Martin, Laura C. *The Folklore of Birds*. Old Saybrook, Conn.: Globe Pequot, 1993.

Simon, Hilda. *The Courtship of Birds*. New York: Dodd, Mead, 1977.

Peterson, Roger Tory. *A Field Guide to the Birds of Eastern and Central North America*. 4th ed. Boston: Houghton Mifflin, 1980.

Reilly, Edgar M. *The Audubon Illustrated Handbook of American Birds*. New York: McGraw-Hill, 1968.

Seabrook, Charles. "Georgia's Disappearing Songbirds," pt. 3. *Atlanta Journal-Constitution*, May 22, 2001, A6.

———. "Wild Georgia." *Atlanta Journal-Constitution*, March 13, 2005, M4.

Thoreau, Henry David. *Walden; or, Life in the Woods*. Boston: Ticknor and Fields, 1854; reprinted in the Dover Thrift Editions series, 1995.

Weidensaul, Scott. *The Birder's Miscellany: A Fascinating Collection of Facts, Figures, and Folklore from the World of Birds*. New York: Fireside/Simon & Schuster, 1991.

White, E. B. *Essays of E. B. White*. New York: Harper & Row, 1977. White's essay "Mr. Forbush's Friends" derives from his reading *Birds of*

Massachusetts and Other New England States, Forbush's three-volume opus magnum — not the abridgment that I make use of.

Young, Martha [Eli Sheppard, pseud.]. *Plantation Bird Legends*. New York: R. H. Russell, 1902, reprinted by the Books for Libraries Press in 1971.

INDEX